Making Sense:
Seventy Western Zen Stories

Michele Lalla

Translated from Italian by the author and
revised by William John Bromwich

D1315390

Dedication

To my wife Maria Paola:

provocative, persistent, and passionate.

To my mother-in-law Clara:

for her encouragement and appreciative comments.

Table of contents

Epigraph

Do not stop at the prologue

but go beyond and follow the dialogue.

Then the path before you

will lead to the end.

Prologue

Bashu, the Master, gathered his disciples and said to them: You are here and do not know why you came. You think you know, but what you believe isn't always right. Go away, then. No? You say now that you are here, you want to stay here and you are here to seek the truth because if you do not, you will be lost. But I tell you that you are already lost while looking for it. The truth is nowhere and those who seek it end up getting lost. If you get lost, you are here without being here. If you do not get lost, you lose the truth, and you are no longer here. Do not get lost. Be resilient. Every time you feel the need to flee, stand firm. Every time you get the urge to stay, flee. Go for the truth which allows you to lose yourselves, but be careful not to lose yourselves. The way not to get lost is resilience. If you are resilient, you will get by. You need strength to seek the truth but only a crazy person can be for the truth, with the truth, in the truth. Go back to where you came from, before getting to the point of no return.

Do not go back but be resilient. Seek the truth, but be aware that it is unattainable. Do not go beyond yourselves and leave no traces. Your wish is to seek the truth in order to understand it and reach its heart, but it has no access. Seeing is an art that you never learn entirely. This art is for the deluded. You are deluded if seek an immutable kernel. What doesn't change is inert and so it is not alive, it is dead. It doesn't go and doesn't come. The truth is immutable because it is beyond coming and going, but it is more alive than dead because it can be achieved only through change. You are mutable in search of immutability, and deluded. There is only the present that offers you your own truth without meaning, hidden by appearances.

You live in a dense fog and need a guide. You seek a guide in the master, whereas the guide is in yourself. You search for the guide in yourself, when the guide is in the master. You cannot solve the dilemma, without dissolving yourselves, but after this dissolution, there is nothing more, because there was never anything along your path. You walked to get to the house where it is possible to learn about life, but once there you find that people live without living, because they are no longer attached to the world. You are in the world but standing outside world. If you want to live, then get out of the school of life. Go and encounter life.

You are in an unstable mental state and are looking for permanent stability, but do not delude yourselves. Stability has a foundation only in instability, in the combination of proposition and opposition. The stability you are looking for is eternity, because it gives you the force of immortality in the form of power. Are you hungry for power? Power will starve you into submission. Only force, without force you are weak. Without power you are dehydrated, like a thirsty soul in the desert. You are power hungry? Power will drown you. What is this force used for? Is it used to run away from your fears or to increase them? No. You want the power to subjugate the world to your will, but power will subjugate you and in the end destroy you. To have power, turn away from power. Otherwise, you will be sick and, as a result, you only need to care. You are ready to care. Be prepared to take a bitter medicine to learn how to appreciate strength and weakness and the honey in everything.

Everything is nothing, because all things are unborn. If all things are unborn, how were you born? This is the first question I ask you. Answer this question and you will find the sense that you are looking for, but only when you no longer seek it, because you are obsessed with making sense out of nonsense, you will look for it obsessively.

The second question I ask follows on from the first. What was your face before you were born? If you are not born, how can there be a birth and then a life? If you are born, what was your face before? Search for a sense of the dilemma and you will gain insight into the meaning of things.

Otherwise you will be confined to the narrow vision of the eyes and not that of the heart. You will be restricted to the sensations of the body and not to the light of the mind. The eyes and the heart, the mind and the body are one thing only. The inner eye will open by oneself, but it is up to you to open your eyelids. Then the body and the mind will resonate in unison and your heart will have eyes.

The third question springs from the mind, which you associate with the head. Some people say that you should not think with your head, but with your navel. This will encourage instinct rather than the head. Where you will go headless nobody will know. Do not leave your head as you may not find it again, but find your head in truth. You already know that nothing can be attained in an unattainable thing. And truth is unattainable. As a result, you are lost again, so you need to think with the mind and the body. Here the question arises. When you do not think with the mind and with the non-mind, who are you really? Answer and you will find the truth that lies beyond the coming and going of thought, beyond the body and the mind.

I have nothing more to tell you: I have told you everything. But I will tell you many stories. From these you may find a way and it will be your way. If you do not find it, there will be no sense because your way is elsewhere. Whoever is lost needs to be resolute. Whoever is not lost needs to be decisive. You still have time to save yourselves by going away. You still have time to find yourselves by staying here to face up to the questions that will lift the veils of ignorance. *Gate, gate, paragate, parasamgate, Bodhi, svaha!*[1]

---

[1] The phrase is written without accents and means, "*O Bodhi, gone, gone, gone on the other riverside, landed at the other riverside, Svaha!*" For the sake of simplicity, the diacritical signs used in transcribing Sanskrit, Chinese, and Japanese terms are eliminated hereinafter. The phrase cited by Bashu comes from the Prajna-paramita-hridaya Sutra. The literature of the Prajna-paramita does not present magic formulae, termed Mantram or Dharani. The

Prajna-paramita-hridaya contains the phrase pronounced by Bashu and represents a rare exception. The formula constitutes a kind of blessing, which concludes a dry speech packed with ideas. In fact, Bashu's speech is dry and full of suggestions. The implications of this statement, that could justify to some extent and in some senses the use made by Bashu to conclude his speech, are described in Suzuki (1977, vol. III, pp. 189-204). Hereinafter, the numbers of volumes and pages of citations refer to the Italian editions.

1. The need for love

"I need love," a man said to Bashu.

"Then, you need to love," Bashu replied.

"How can I love someone, if no-one loves me?"

"How can someone love you, if you are not able to love? Therefore, learn to love."

2. Loneliness along with others

"Where does loneliness come from?" a monk asked Bashu.

"It comes from the ability to get together with others," Bashu said to him.

"I know about being together with others," pressed the monk. "But I still feel alone."

"A man who knows about being together with others is not alone."

3. Suffering and happiness

"Why do we suffer?" a student asked Bashu.

"To be happy," Bashu said to him.

"How can someone be happy if he is suffering?" he insisted.

"I never said that someone who suffers is happy, but you cannot be happy without having experienced suffering," Bashu answered him patiently.

"Of course, but would it not be better, if we could enjoy happiness without experiencing unhappiness?" the disciple went on, with a glimmer of hope in his eyes.

Then came the response. "Would it not be better to carry on sleeping, instead of waking up every morning?"

4. The meaning of life and the end

"I wake up at night and think of the wonders of the world. Then, I think everything will come to an end and I cry about this transient life. I mourn life that is running away. Master, why is all this happening?" a disciple in distress asked Bashu.

"You think too much and live too little," Bashu replied.

"Must not people think, then?" the disciple snapped back.

"People must live," Bashu answered him simply.

"Is not thought the origin of action, and is not action the origin of life?"

"The origin of life is to live."

"Where is the meaning of life, master, if it all ends?"

"Where is life, if everything ends before living a life?"

5. Losing is finding

"I reflect on the transience of being and I am sad for the futility of days swallowed up by time. Then, Master, I do not understand the essence of life and I lose myself in the inevitable loss of time," a disciple confided in Bashu.

"Time is not lost, because time is you yourself."

"If I am time, then should it not get lost with me?" the disciple asked ardently.

"Are you a lost man, perhaps?"

"No, I am not lost today, but tomorrow I will be part of something else and I will no longer be myself. I will be transformed, but I will lose the identity I have today."

"Transforming yourself does not mean being part of something else, nor losing your identity."

"Yes, but I am sad at the thought of no longer being what I am now," the disciple concluded and added, "I want to stay here in the present."

"Those who stop are those who really die. Those who are alive are moving and changing as time goes by."

"Master, this blind following of the flow of time makes me sad."

"Follow it with your eyes wide open."

"How can I follow it, even with my eyes open, if I am forced to give up today all that I love and wish to keep forever, like a present?"

"Here is the rub. You can keep what you have only by giving it up. And you can live in the present by accepting it and adapting to change, losing something to find something else."

6. A smile to die

Naturami became a disciple of Bashu at an advanced age, and was one of the first. His eccentricity became evident almost immediately: listening with rapture to the words of the master, contemplating the sunsets for hours, waiting for the sunrise with trepidation, tending the garden with devotion. However, his serenity faded away after contemplation and meditation, as his concentration on emptiness made him feel in a void. He got lost in the absence of ideas and emotions, and he received nothing from his efforts. Thinking about emptiness made him empty but it did not change anything in him. He just remained empty. Contemplating a drop of water or a grain of sand, however, filled him with serenity. He complained about this, because he became convinced that he was incapable of self-understanding, thought, and the mind. As a result, he gave up, disillusioned, and returned to his usual occupations.

In his old age one day he realized he was dying and sent someone to call Bashu. He wanted to show him his gratitude for the teachings received. Bashu came promptly, "Naturami, today your absence will give us your presence in unity and joy."

"Thank you, Master, for the joy that you give me. The end is long anticipated, but I have not fulfilled my task. I die in ignorance. Maybe I should regret this but, instead, I face the end in a happy state of mind." With tenderness Bashu hugged him strongly, saying, "You were what you were and this is enough. You have been yourself in your absolute present."

After hearing these words up from within, he managed just to whisper, "Thank you Master, now I understand everything," and died with a smile on his face in the loving arms of Bashu.

7. Understanding nothingness

After lunch Bashu was in the habit of taking leave of his disciples and retired to meditate. One day, one of them followed him and waited for him behind the door, while the master was meditating. The disciple walked away only before Bashu came out. This scene was repeated throughout the week and Bashu pretended not to notice. The disciple continued to follow and watch the afternoon meditations of the master even over the following weeks.

Once Bashu came across him asleep in a position that stopped him from leaving room, and then waited for him to wake up. The disciple, embarrassed when he saw his master, threw himself at his feet apologizing for his behaviour. His embarrassment gave him the strength to express his doubts, "Master, I wanted to talk to you, but I did not dare. I am sorry for my disappointing results. What to do? I listen but do not hear anything. I look and do not see anything. I think and my mind does not think anything. How can I continue to stay here and not learn anything?"

"Perseverance helps learning."

"Can I learn if I do not understand anything?"

"Can you understand nothing and want to learn?"

"Maybe, maybe not. I do not know, but I know that I want to leave," the dejected disciple said.

"If that is what you want, that is what you should do. But before leaving, I beg you to do me a favour. Continue to watch over my afternoon meditation for a month. In the end, if you are of the same opinion, you can leave."

The last afternoon of the month, the disciple was there, sitting behind the door with a decisive look. He greeted the master haughtily and told him, "Nothing has changed in me. It is better for me to leave."

"So be it," Bashu exclaimed. The disciple, who had already packed away his belongings, made his way towards

21

the door. As he crossed the threshold, Bashu addressed him, "If you do not understand anything, you will go on to encounter nothing." The disciple turned his face full of dismay, "I will go to meet nothing and drown in nothing." A scream rang out through the air.

"Aaah! If you do not understand anything, you cannot even drown in anything. To understand nothing is to understand everything." The tone of voice, even more than the comment, pierced him from side to side and nailed him to the door. He could not cross the doorstep, but came back. It was like a cry that stopped in the throat and neither fell nor rose. He had to make a huge effort to move because he was paralyzed. He seemed to jump out, but he fell back. He jumped in, but he seemed to jump out. Any superabundance of force generates its opposite, and this enantiodromia led to his loss in space and time, a feeling of disorientation that tore at the veil of ignorance and the vision of truth. Two circular movements embraced him: To fill and empty himself, to drain and fill, to fill and drain, which cleared up his confusion, and an unexpected light, dim though it was, filled his heart.

8. An eclectic man

A young man was called Kogamo (duckling) by his friends because of he was short and stocky, with short crooked legs. They used this nickname in a friendly way, though at times intending to ridicule, but he always responded with a smile because his gentle nature made him prone to tolerance. His smile of those occasions was in sharp contrast with his inflexible temper at other times. His eccentric character led him to criticize the contradictions of real life and spiritual life. His thirst for truth made him seek knowledge in the teachings of itinerant preachers. As a result, he tended towards eclecticism. He reflected on their teachings and at times took issue with the preachers. How could he fathom their understanding, if their words were not fit for purpose? Everyone could achieve holiness in an exemplary life, but without the knowledge of the truth, what could they accomplish? For him only knowledge was a source of salvation. He became convinced that a limited being, like man, could not fathom nature that was unlimited. Knowledge was a return to ignorance. Certain knowledge implied the end of everything.

"Who would be saved, if everything would end in nothing?" He replied to himself, "Only those who achieve enlightenment can save themselves from nothing and transcend the cycle of birth and death." He knew that not many people would be saved, only a few. Out of a sense of justice, which was alien to his environment, he did not accept that the good things were reserved only for a few, while others, who were the majority, would search in vain for truth and enlightenment. It was necessary to gain salvation for everyone, but it had to be accessible to all and easy to achieve. He was going around in circles. To break the vicious circle of his reasoning, he repeated to himself, "Yes, it is available to everyone, but it requires commitment and perseverance within the limits of the self. These limits are obstacles because they lead us astray or make us give up easily. Without limits, there is nothing, and transcending these limits leads to liberation." There are those who argued that salvation was for everyone, it was enough to have faith. They claimed that the truth will set you free (John 8.32); but truth and freedom were elusive and, sometimes, in contrast with each other.

Many people live in slavery because "there is nothing equal to wearing clothes and eating food".[2]

He had not yet seen people survive without food and clothes. Still, the starting point of that profound insight, which racked his brain leading him to breaking point, was in the verse: *To save a life, you have to destroy it.*[3]

He left his family and travelled through the world because he wanted to destroy the life he had led up to then. In this way he hoped to find salvation. He wanted to find the Way, the Truth, and the Light. He longed to find the source of a faith that he did not know because he had heard that, "*Whoever believes in me will be saved*" (Matthew 9.22, Mark 5.34, Luke 17.19, John 3.16).

He travelled extensively in the villages. He held various jobs. He suffered hunger, thirst, and cold. He lost himself among the stars and found himself in a violet. He flowed into the river and returned to the sea. He fell asleep on the grass

---

[2] Verse of the Zenrin (Watts, 1957, p. 164). The Zenrin Kushu is an anthology of 5000 couplets, compiled by Toyo Eicho (1429-1504) with the aim of providing documentation from which to choose poetic couplets dealing with the theme of a new koan resolved. The couplets were taken from various Chinese sources (Taoist and Buddhist literature and tradition).

[3] Verse of the Zenrin (Watts, 1957, p. 165). Something similar is to be found in John (12.24-25): "**24** *I tell you the truth, unless a kernel of wheat falls to the ground and dies, it remains only a single seed. But if it dies, it produces many seeds.* **25** *The man who loves his life will lose it, while the man who hates his life in this world will keep it for eternal life*".

and woke up in the wind. He stared at the moon and worshipped the sun. Finally Kogamo decided to join a school, as he failed to find fulfillment in his itinerant life. He asked Bashu if he could join his school, and Bashu allowed him to. He hoped to talk to Bashu, but he was sent to the kitchen to wash the pots and the floors. He wanted to rebel against this humiliating treatment, but it was his choice and he wished to see where he would arrive. A year went by and he was still there washing the pots. One day he decided to take Bashu to task. "Master, I have been here for a year and you haven't taught me anything. Can you tell me when the teaching will start?"

"The kitchen door is here and the exit is there," Bashu told him. So Kogamo returned to the kitchen and decided that he would work for another year. Then he would have resumed wandering life. He spent his time after work unravelling the thread of his skein, from empty to full, from the existence of non-existence to the transience of thought, from the reconciliation of right and wrong to the destruction of the harmony of opposites. At the end of the second year he went back to Bashu and was determined to tell him clearly that if Bashu did not begin to teach him Zen, he would leave. The response of Bashu, however, was still the same, "The kitchen door is here and the exit is there."

Kogamo said goodbye, determined to head for the exit, but when he was on the threshold, Bashu took his stick to beat the gong three times. The loud noise confused Kogamo, who found himself heading towards the kitchen. He continued like an automaton to the threshold of kitchen. There he stopped for a moment and turned to Bashu, saying,

"The soup is ready,
the smell has gone away,
nothing is left."

Bashu said,

"Nothing is empty,
nothing on fire.
    The Lotus Flower burns to ashes."

Kogamo continued,

"Ashes in the wind
feed the ground
    and roots, then complete a cycle."

After a moment, Kogamo added, "There is something in me of which I know nothing; but it lives, it manifests itself, and I am at one with it. What it is, I do not care about as the main interest in it now is to live."

"The truth is in you and all doors are open to you," Bashu concluded, dismissing him.

9. The father of a son in flight

Yosa was the only son of a wealthy family. As a child, he was intolerant of orders, disobeying instructions, answering back to his parents, protesting with his teachers for teachings that he did not like, starting quarrels with his teammates at times for trivial reasons. He grew susceptible and skittish, moody and grumpy. He walked like a bird in the yard. His family and friends then gave him the nickname Kari (wild goose). He liked it. He had a good heart in the end, but a very bad temper that made his parents feel powerless in his upbringing. His father, Sekimori, wanted to hand over his business to him at some time in the future, but Kari always said that he was not interested in the wealth of his father because he just wanted to be himself. This alarmed and offended Sekimori, because the boy kept his distance from the poorest, though they were the source of his wealth. He sent Kari to an elite school far away from his home to remove him from the contrast between rich and poor, to prepare him for the future management of the family business, and to deal with his rebellious nature.

His parents waited patiently for their son's behaviour to improve. Initially no improvement was apparent because Kari's interests were varied and changed over time. Later his exuberance gave way to contemplation, his impatience subsided into equanimity, pride was replaced by humility, and his wildness was softened by affability. But the rebellious streak was firmly entrenched. One day Kari left his school and gave no more news of his whereabouts. His parents were in dismay, his mother cried for not having loved him enough, his father reproached himself for not understanding his temperament and for not finding the keys to his heart and to set him on the right path. Finally, after days of pain and anguish his father decided he would look for Kari for as long as he lived. He handed over the management

27

of his business to his two daughters, who seemed interested and capable, but this was a strong and courageous decision, and not in line with tradition. Sekimori said goodbye to his wife and daughters, and set off.

Sekimori began the search for Kari by walking the streets of nearby villages and towns, the trails of the mountains and lakes, the schools of the Zen masters. He found no trace of Kari, but some monks had noticed a young man listening to the teachings of their masters who matched the description given to them by Sekimori. He did not lose heart and continued his fearless search. His feet hurt, his clothes were torn, his strength was giving way, but his thoughts became clearer and clearer. He was determined to continue the search for Kari, although he feared he might not recognize Kari any more due to the changes in his appearance. In his wanderings Sekimori discovered many things he thought he knew, but really he did not know: poverty suffered by men with patience, the abjection that turned them into wolves, the needs that made them slaves, the pain that humiliated them and made them impotent, the mutilation that offended them in their desires. Among this suffering humanity he began to be ashamed of the wealth of the past, to understand the reasons (unexpressed and perceived) of his child, to justify his running away. He saw shame and abjection in his own past. He felt confusion and despair in the present. What was the point of all the tricks he used to increase his earnings? What was the point of his life spent in cotton wool like a silkworm? What had he learned of his true needs in those years? What was the primary good of his heart? In the obsession of the questions, the search for Kari was his guiding star in order not to be overwhelmed by despair and shame.

His supreme good was just this attempt to find, or rather to find himself. He was aware that his strength was running out. Maybe it was useless to look around without looking inside, a real insight. He needed help to go into depth, he needed a guide. One day he decided, therefore, to stop and to stay at a school with a teacher to be reassured, to learn the necessary things, even though he was afraid of not having enough time to do it. There he meditated on the sound of one hand clapping, the emptiness in a clenched fist, and the fullness of emptiness. The deep understanding of the koan[4] did not appease the desire to search for the authentic self, but all his self was the search for Kari.

He had understood and this is what he needed to do. He was a prisoner of his own goals. So he began the search again and wandered the streets he had walked down so many times, meeting people he had known. Now, a greeting or a nod was enough to communicate a movement of the soul, an act of kindness, a wish. He could not give away very much, but he shared everything he had with those who were in need. His smiles were flashes of serenity, which passed spontaneously from him to them, and felt a return of fullness from them to him and from him to them. His movements became slow and solemn, his gaze serene, his face relaxed, and he had a pleasant air. The atmosphere of warm hospitality emerged without visible signs, but with an instinctive empathy that was being formed with others. Sekimori was old and no longer had much strength. He needed to settle down in a permanent home, but he could not stop and slowly continued his journey to meet his destiny.

One day fatigue got the better of him. He stopped, overcome with tiredness on the street corner of a slum and he realized that he did not have long to live. Yet still he listened with strained attention to what was happening around him, and he thought of his son, who had given him the strength to get away, to get lost to find himself, to give up everything to accept anything that was all, to suffer for the joy of true love.

---

[4] Koan is the theme, the dilemma, the antinomy on which to meditate to overcome the absurdity of the content and to reach a site beyond common sense. Originally, it meant "principle of government". Today it means "principle of eternal truth" transmitted by the master (Deshimaru, 1977a, p. 192), but here it is often considered as a contradictory issue of existence.

Suddenly Sekimori heard a voice that touched his heart and he knew that it was the voice of his Kari. "Sweet and beloved Kari, I am now coming to you." A force startled him, he found his voice, and rejoined his Kari, who was there like an apparition, "Kari, my son," and opened his arms. Kari turned around. He was surprised to see his father slowly approaching like a bird in flight. Light and dance, shining clouds and fragile wings in his steps. Kari saw himself in those sunken and radiant eyes, in that scarred and happy face, which resembled his own. He saw himself in that life imprinted in those gestures as an authentic being who had found himself. This was state that Kari had claimed to pursue as a young man. The destiny that Kari followed was before his eyes: The dancing steps and the open arms of his father unfolded in the motion of a tender embrace as well as the truth buried by money and conventions or the feelings suffocated by appearance and presumption. Kari's face was the younger copy of Sekimori's old face.

"Father, I beg your forgiveness ...."

"Kari, do not say anything. Once for all, it is finished. Thank you for the strength you have given me in this journey. I have reached my destination and now it is I who have to ask you for forgiveness." Kari interrupted him with determination, "No, I was the one who went away without saying a word, but I could not ...." He wanted to say more, even though he knew they did not need words to understand each other. Total understanding permeated them. There was a brief silence, like a lifetime pulsating in enlightenment, because Sekimori had finally found the eternal and inviolable way, "Thank you again son. Now I can rejoin and be happy with nature. Embrace me: I am going to die," and with a calm expression he passed away in the arms of Kari.

10. To speak and to be silent

"Can someone talk about something by not talking about it?" a wayfarer asked Bashu.

"Can someone to be silent by not being silent?" Bashu replied, pulling himself up straight.

11. The discipline of stick

Usaki Kusatao was a Zen master who made his students to endure an iron discipline. During meditation, it was strictly forbidden to arouse even the slightest suspicion of distraction. The attendant, who was often the master himself, approached the disciple, greeted him with a ceremonious bow, and then with the Keisaku dealt a decisive blow on the right shoulder of the disciple. Among themselves, behind his back, the disciples called this behaviour "the harsh law of Keisaku."[5]

Every little mistake in action and words was equally punished. Usaki Kusatao did not say almost anything, he did not converse with his disciples, he did not make speeches, and education of disciples was not directly explanatory. As a result, some of the disciples called this method "the path of silence to satori."[6]

---

[5] Keisaku is a wooden warning stick, round at one end and flattened to the other. It was the symbol of the sword of prajna of the Bodhisattva Manjusri (Watts, 1957, p. 169). It is used during the period of meditation to deal with sleepiness or lapses of concentration. The term is also transcribed kyosaku (Deshimaru, 1977a, p. 192) and in this case the common translation is "encouragement stick".

[6] Satori, in Chinese tun-wu, indicates the sudden awakening achieved by the pupil of the school with a single flash of insight, without going through the preparatory stages. Satori denotes the awakening to the cosmic truth. The awakening is also the Way (Bodhi), the enlightenment, the reality. Another name for satori is kensho, "seeing into one's true nature" (Suzuki, 1950, p. 60). On seeing his own nature the individual is put into a state of consciousness, where there is neither the subject nor the object, so he/she can be only in a state of absolute empty, devoid of meaning for his/her life, which pulsates emotions and expectations or may be tormented by suffering and frustration. This line of thought is

The severity of the rules was unbearable for many, and they ended up dropping out of school. They had to endure at the time of their departure also the last and harder beating. They had to suffer, even then, the silence of the master: not a word, not a smile, not a greeting. The stick spoke for him. Only the more fearful, timid, and obedient disciples remained there. Only those who could not bear the shame of failure, in returning home, passively suffered harassment. Only a few disciples forged their character, but everyone continued to sleep while half-waking.

Kaneko Fusei did not approve of the punitive and uneducated conduct of his master, but he did not want to go on to other masters before achieving his goal. This justified the laziness of the heart, the faults of others incited him to surrender, the adversity was something he had to face. He was there and there he must remain. There was the end and the beginning. There was the obstacle to be overcome in order to achieve his aim. Zen was there and now. Sometimes, Kaneko closed his eyes and forgot the rest. The more concentrated he was, the more easily he deceived the overseer. The more effortlessly he deceived the overseer, the more simply he became lost in his absence. The more readily he vanished in his absence, the more clearly he discovered the presence of being. Time passed and nothing happened to him, as he sank into the sleep of the senses and reason. Time passed and permeated his mind and his senses. One morning he got up and realized that his place was no longer there. He had absolutely to go away to find the true way. Kaneko Fusei went to Usaki Kusatao, but he did not succeed in opening his mouth and then received a thrashing. He stood there trying to speak aloud and fast, "Master, I want to learn and so I want to go." Usaki Kusatao brandished the stick at hit him, but

---

dual because satori is an individual and concrete experience, which goes to the foundations of reason to penetrate the non-differentiated whole, to attain the vision of the "suchness of things" that summarizes the two contradictory concepts of empty and full (Suzuki, 1950, p. 62-63).

Kaneko grabbed the stick and broke it in two pieces with a sharp blow. The teacher remained with a piece of stick in his hands, like a king with a broken sceptre.

"How do you get permission to do that?" Usaki shouted.

"How do you get permission to do that?" Kaneko answered.

"Go away, you ill-mannered good-for-nothing" Usaki growled, trying to hit him with the stump that remained in his hand. However, as Kaneko swerved, Usaki's arm ended up on Kaneko's shoulder and the stump fell to the ground. There was a deep frost between them and both were drowning in the water of silence. After a while, Kaneko began to say defiantly,

> *"The stick misleads*
> *and restarts the motion*
> > *you go standing still.*
> > > *You stand still and go*
> > > *no one can stop in line*
> > > *the motion time."*

With a deep bow Kaneko took his leave of Usaki and went away. Later, he founded a school renowned for the harmony between students and teacher, for intense and insightful dialogues stimulated by the strength of his personality. As a result, he had many successors.

12. The old age of letters

A disciple devoted to reading confided in Bashu one day, "Master, almost everything that has been written seems to be a reworking of what has already been said or written before."

"That can only be a good thing," Bashu replied. Almost ignoring the remark, the disciple objected, "Repetition creates an unbearable feeling of being old."
"You risk not being able to face your old age," Bashu responded, not without malice.

"Ageing is the absence of that which is new," the disciple said.

"The new becomes old immediately after you have read it, but if the reader reworks it, it adds depth, it enhances your understanding; so it is new," Bashu answered.

"You mean that it is like the water in a river? It runs down into the sea, then evaporates, then falls as rain into the source, and runs again through the same point. It is always new, but it is always old. If this is so, then the problem is how to gain understanding," the disciple went on.

"Now is the time to learn to forget what you have learned," Bashu concluded, with a smile that warmed the heart of his disciple.[7]

---

[7] The closure relates in some way to a comment written by an anonymous reader of the Zen story "*A cup, a vacuum*" (Deshimaru , 1983, p. 16), which is identical to "*Time to die*" (Senzaki, Reps, 1957, pp. 93-94). An anonymous reader wrote in the book of the library Antonio Delfini an evaluation with a note, "*Zero. It seems to me the story of Chicchibio*" (Boccaccio, 1976 vol. II, the sixth day, the fourth novel, pp. 109-112). The remark shows a mistaken approach to Zen literature. Yet, reading the version of Taisen Deshimaru, one has the impression resulting in a similar comment. Anyone familiar with both versions can verify that there is a negligible difference in style between the two ways of telling the story. Taisen Deshimaru is redundant, twisted, rhetorical, overly

13. Speaking to make noise

A layman, coming across Bashu, said, "Master, you monks have abandoned your parents. You are not married. You have no children. You do not perform any work. You are out in this world. You study and talk about your studies, you meditate and live on donations. It is too convenient for you." Bashu quickened his step, but the other went on, insisting, "For you it is easier."

"Yes, it is true, it is easier for us," Bashu admitted. Surprised by the admission, he continued to follow him, asking, "Why is it denied us to achieve enlightenment?"

"No one has denied you enlightenment. You are denying yourself."

"How can I deny myself what I cannot do? It is impossible for me to sit in meditation, to refine contemplation aimed at releasing the prajna. Finally, after releasing prajna, I may discover my true nature. How is it possible? I need a commitment to follow this procedure, but I cannot practice it. What should I do then?"

"Do well what you do. Be yourself and carry on your business, act as one with it," Bashu suggested in a patient and kindly manner.

---

sophisticated; while Nyogen Senzaki and Paul Reps are concise, direct, essential, immediate and simple. The effect on the reader is the opposite, while Deshimaru seems to lack spontaneity, Senzaki and Reps convey the sense of spontaneity even with a trivial device, used perhaps to avoid a reprimand. Immediacy is the essence of Zen to be found also in a witty remark. The disciples were trained to express themselves in support of a position on complex subjects in adversarial proceedings. See in this respect "*Dialogue Zen*" in Nyogen Senzaki and Paul Reps (1957, no. 89, pp. 96-97).

"You speak in a difficult way to get round the problem. How can I be myself and love when I love, work when I work, rest when I rest, and play when I play?" the layman persisted. "Every day I worry there may not be anything to eat in the evening."

"And you do not need to worry there may not be anything to eat in the evening."

"How can you talk like that, when you ask the community?"

"How can you be silent, when you talk just to hear the sound of your own voice?" Bashu replied dismissively.

14. The way of the wind

An eccentric monk said to Bashu, "Master, I like to listen to the wind. It caresses your hair. It charms you with its eyes and enchants you with its moaning. I follow it like a child follows the kite: in heaven and on earth, over the mountain and down the valley, on the streets and in the squares; but I always lose myself because it has no direction."

"The wind has a direction," Bashu said.

"Yes, but it changes often," he went on with a discouraged tone, "First you see it in a gully, then in a clearing, then blowing from the north, then from the south. Master, the wind goes round in circles."

"You turn round. The wind turns for the wind," said Bashu with a bow, and took his leave.

15. Be worthy of your thoughts alone

An itinerant monk stopped in a village. Among those listening to him, there was a boy, who followed him totally engrossed, with the eyes of a newborn calf. The following evening there was only that one little boy listening to him. After waiting a short time, the monk told the boy there was nobody else to listen to him and, as a result, he would not talk just for him.

"Why won't you talk?" the boy answered, "Are you worth less than your pride?"

"No," the monk replied quietly. "You are worth less than my time devoted to meditation."

"If there had been more people, you would have spoken. That means many are worth more than one," the boy replied.

"Yes, because only one is worth more than many, and none is worth yourself," the monk said.

"Of course," the boy answered, blinking again like a newborn calf, "I see that only your thoughts are worth something in principle, but they are not worth listening to, if there is just one person to listen. You can remain alone with your thoughts," said the boy as he walked away.

18. The illusion of the truth

"Is there only one self? Or are there many selves? At every moment I feel different, as if I were another, yet they are always me. Where is the truth?" a novice asked Bashu.

"In the bread you eat," he answered.

"Master, when I eat, is it me that welcomes the bread or is the bread that welcomes me?"

"Is it your mouth that speaks words or is it the words that speak your mouth?" Bashu jested.

"Oh! Master, I am confused. My mouth does not speak without words and my words cannot be spoken without my mouth. Knowledge is equal to ignorance faced with the illusory nature of truth, the senses and the world. What should I do?"

"Put your shoes over your eyes and walk."

19. To cry and to laugh

Taiga was a lively, curious, and precocious child. After listening to the preaching of a Zen monk, he asked his parents to go to school. Initially, they opposed his demands and paid a private tutor for a few years. At the age of twelve, after insisting so strongly and with conviction, Taiga was granted the permission of his parents to attend the Zen school of Bashu.

His progress at school was amazing, and in his studies of Buddhism he learned effortlessly. He achieved concentration as he controlled his body and mind with ease, and in dialogues he was extremely perspicacious. The achievement of enlightenment was not, however, easy at all, despite his determination and commitment. He experienced the feeling of weightlessness and beyond his mind. He swirled in invisible circles, staring at the serene blue sky. He perceived the cosmic substance permeating his whole body. He could be conscious in his sleep, detached in his waking, unflappable in his desire. He went along with his flow of thoughts in empty space sinking in absence. Many times he was close to awakening, and yet he was stopped by a barrier that was almost imperceptible. The futility of the sound of one hand clapping, the senselessness of the emptiness of a clenched fist, the inconsistency of standing up to sit down, the absurdity penetrating into the sound of sound, the impossibility of knowing the face he possessed before birth did not discourage him. But his refractoriness and scepticism in practice prevented him from the awakening. The teacher always encouraged him to go beyond the words, "To sit to cut" (Deshimaru, 1977a , p. 64).

One autumn day he sat in meditation under a persimmon tree, with the intent of staying there until he became aware of an appreciable result. After one full day, he fell into a state between wakefulness and sleep: A mixture of watchfulness and absence. On the second day a storm broke, but Taiga stood there motionless, and not even the heavy thunder shook him. Suddenly a persimmon broke off and fell on his head. That soft and sticky feeling moved him to enlightenment, revealing to him the mystery of death and life. He came back and wrote the following verses.

The search led by the mind
grappled in the web of words.

Even the desire for truth
you had to leave behind. Calmly waiting
I sat in the shade of a persimmon tree.

The flash upon me did not light my way
nor did thunder wake me from sleep
but only the blow on the head of ripe fruit.

The master had reached the limits of his teaching, but Taiga, carried away by his enthusiasm, wanted to improve himself and decided to stay and continue under his guidance.

One day Taiga's father came to beg him to leave the monastic life because his sister and brother had died. His mother and father alone could not carry on their business and wanted to find him a wife. Faced with Taiga's refusal, his father burst into tears of despair. Taiga went into a room to meditate and the distressed father settled himself down not far from the door of the room and waited in silence. On the third day his father had not moved and Taiga was still inside the room. His friends told the master of what was happening. Bashu went to Taiga, saying, "You experienced the joy of enlightenment. Now, you are facing the reality of the world, and a duty that you cannot always escape from. Then, even marriage has its importance. The choice is stark but all roads lead to the Road."

Taiga agreed, then, to heed the advice of his father. He went home, got married and became the father of two boys and one girl. At the age of eight, the eldest son became ill and died. Great was the grief of Taiga. A few days after the burial, a disconsolate weeping overcame him. A neighbour who caught him crying rebuked him, "You should not cry! As the pupil of the great master Bashu, how can you let yourself go to such weakness? How can you be desperate, if you understand the essence of life and death? Is it not a shame?"

"Do not worry about the essence of life and death," said Taiga. "This is my Zen: To cry, when you need to cry, and to laugh, when you need to laugh."[9]

---

[9] The structure of the story brings to mind "*Buddhism and the World*" (Cleary, 1993, pp. 89-91), but here the contents and moods, though criticized by Zen Buddhism as impediments to free intuition, are different from those of that story. In addition, the final answer can bring to mind the final proposition in Bankei "The real miracle" (Senzaki, Reps, 1957, p. 90), but the usual caveat applies.

the contingent state, beyond thought, beyond matter, beyond passion.[10]

Naruse crossed the threshold after Yamazaki attacked him. Yamazaki fell at his feet begging for forgiveness. Naruse picked him up, hugged him, and sent him away without saying a word. Yamazaki went to Gassen and told him what had happened and asked him to give the kesa[11] to Naruse and let him go for the world. Gassen said, "Go and follow your destiny. Envy has distracted you from the truth. Pain will bring you down difficult paths, but fruitful for you, at the end of which you will find yourself and also find peace." Yamazaki took his leave with a deep bow, and walked away: His step was light, like a cornflower in the field, like a flamingo in flight, like a turtle in motion. In his travel diary he wrote the following verses.

> *I do not know where I will go*
> *Today, clouds of mud*
>   *are upon me.*

> *The wind whips*
> *eyes turned upward*
>   *before, and now at the bottom,*

---

[10] Naruse's answer seems to evoke Bankei's answer in "Readiness" (Cleary, 1993, p. 30). The similarities and the differences remind us of the intertwining of Christian values with Zen Buddhism. This story might also bring to mind the rivalry between Hui-neng and Shen-hsiu, that was probably invented (Suzuki, 1977, vol. I, pp. 193-197).

[11] Kesa is the habit of the Buddha, in Japanese, kasaya in Sanskrit. It is the habit of the Buddhist monks and nuns, the symbol of the transmission from master to disciple. The seams of the robe replicate the design of a paddy field. The design of the habit thus evokes work in the paddy fields in the beauty of the fabric, pointing out that even the worst can become better and the profane may have a sacred side (Deshimaru, 1977a, p. 192).

but the feet are
careful not to tread on
violets in the street.

Yamazaki's journey was long and tiring. He wandered aimlessly. At every step a staging place materialized unexpectedly, like the wood in spring that suddenly turns green. Defeat did not call for redemption, but gave rise to shame! There was nothing to be redeemed in an action which, fortunately, did not cause any damage. He did not need to prove anything. Rather, shame generated a state of despair and distrust. Where could he lay his head now? The fox had its hole, the bear had its cave, the bird had its nest; but he did not know which way to turn (Luke 9.58). He was desperate not because of the lost opportunity, but due to the heavy load that had landed on him heavier than an avalanche, due to the presumption which had thrown him headlong from the cliff into the abyss, the pride which had crushed him and had broken his flight, the envy which had annihilated his aspirations. He needed a teacher to get back on the right path.

After walking a long way, without a destination in mind, he reached the monastery of Bashu. There he stopped and asked to be allowed in. Suffering intensely, he showed his pain. How could he have committed an act so insane? How could he have been overwhelmed by the mania for power? How much could his insane pride have made him come under thumb of envy? Bashu only said, "Now you know that the bear lives in you, and is not yet tamed, you can wallow in your suffering. You did not know it at that time. Go and work in the laundry." Yamazaki worked hard. His companions gave him, as by common agreement, the more tedious tasks. He felt he was the lowest of the low and was living like a ghost, ignored and never taken into consideration, as if he did not exist. In this state of anonymity, he found joy in serving others and the world rather than himself. It was an act of humiliation that was necessary, not atonement, but an act of humility.

One day Bashu said to his disciples, "You have to wash the kesa. If there is no kesa, what do you wash?" All of them understood this to be an invitation to a competition to stimulate the emergence of the doubt. The next day he found a sign hanging on the door of the dojo that read, "The kesa is the habit of the Buddha, the Buddha does not get dirty, so there is no kesa to wash." All those who read the sign were impressed. Yamazaki said to himself, "The washing of the kesa implies another type of washing. You wash the nothing that becomes everything. There is no more transmission of inheritance, but purification of pride only." Bashu, who heard his softly-spoken words, invited him to speak. After complete silence, he said, "I gave away my kesa. I can only wash my conscience." Bashu replied, "Your pilgrimage is over. The Way is waiting for you. You can go," and he dismissed him forever.

22. Lust

"Why do not you get married?" the young Tombo (dragonfly) asked Bashu. Instead of answering, he sat up straight and looked away. Vexed and disappointed, Tombo continued, "Please, answer me. Why do not you answer me?"

"Ask a silly question, get a silly answer," Bashu said.

"Master, it is not silly because a dilemma torments me. I always want to make love."

"Then do so, if this is your heart's desire."

"But it is sin!" the young Tombo exclaimed.

"It is a sin to stifle genuine needs."

"No, master, it is an uncontrollable desire that seizes me. It is lust," Tombo concluded.

"The words are yours," said Bashu.

"Yes they are, but I am not so sure, or, perhaps, I would like to hear you tell me it is not true. Please, give me some advice, I beg you."

"Try to figure out if it is true and try temperance" Bashu suggested. Young Tombo went away satisfied, intending to strike a balance in his passions.

One day, Tombo met a good-looking woman and could not resist courting her. He knew that she wanted him, she called him without speaking, she longed for him while pretending not to. All presumptuous men thought so, but he was certain that what he perceived was true. He courted her. He flattered her, but it was no more difficult than other conquests because almost immediately he found an enthusiastic and passionate response. However, the woman, whose name was Hotaru, or firefly, was married and they had to see each other in secret, but in this way the whole thing seemed more exciting and intriguing. As time went by, their desire became more and more intense, so each time they ran more and more risks and were less and less careful. One day they met in Hotaru's bedroom because her husband was supposed to be away but due to an unexpected event, he came home much earlier than usual and caught them in the act. Tombo managed to escape from her husband, who was chasing him, brandishing a dagger. The husband chased him to take revenge, but fell while running down the stairs and killed himself with his own dagger. Hotaru fled with Tombo. If she had stayed at home, she would not have escaped the punishment for her wrongdoing, concerning both adultery and the consequent death of her husband. Her son stayed behind with her husband's family.

For a time, running away and living in secret was difficult, but love and passion filled their souls with joy. Lust faded as day-to-day routine took over but Hotaru still attracted him, her smiles distracted him from other women. Their days were full of love. Their joy made them more compassionate with others, assuaging their feelings of guilt. They spent a wonderful period together, with passion, feeling, empathy and sharing. Hotaru got pregnant and gave birth to a child. Everything was like a fascinating dream. Then fate dealt a terrible blow, that had a devastating effect on their marriage. At the age of five, their child died suddenly. Their desperation was great, and despite their great love, Hotaru was overcome by grief and passed away. Tombo lived alone for a while and had no more desire. The sole purpose of his life was to help others.

One day, a strong, sturdy young man appeared, presented himself to Tombo and claimed to be Imai, the son of Hotaru. He had come to avenge the death of his father. Before taking his revenge, however, he wanted to know why Tombo had behaved in such a way. Tombo knelt at his feet without a word and bowed his head, exposing his neck. Imai insisted on an answer, but his words were useless. Out of anger, he decided to go ahead. He was brandishing his sword to strike Tombo, when there was a strong earthquake. The young man lost his balance, fell and hurt himself on his sword. It was a serious injury that rendered him incapable of carrying out his revenge. Tombo decided to nurse him back to health.

After a few weeks, Imai had recovered, so Tombo asked him to postpone his revenge for a few days, in order to help the villagers. He worked day and night for more than a month. He shifted rubble, procured water, consoled the orphans and repaired the damaged huts. Day and night Tombo and the villagers worked together. Meanwhile, Imai did not intend to wait any longer to fulfil his mission and Tombo knew his intentions, so one morning he got up, he approached Imai, and said, "I am ready, here I am." Imai was shocked and surprised by this attitude and continued to ask him to talk about his mother and the reasons that led him to commit adultery. Tombo was silent, head bowed, waiting for the fatal blow.

"I cannot do it," all of a sudden Imai shouted. "You have taken care of me. You helped the villagers. Why should you be guilty of the death of my father? Talk!" The silence of Tombo was immense and Imai, alone and distraught, began to cry. Then Tombo said, "You are always part of events around you, even indirectly. I am responsible for the death of your father, as I am responsible for your injuries. Go on, do your duty." Imai stopped sobbing, but the tears were still running down his face and the hands gripping the sword trembled.

"I cannot. I cannot," he shouted and, throwing down his sword, he went away. Tombo got up and went back to the school of Bashu. He met the master and asked, "Who am I?"

"A young man full of lust," said Bashu.

"It all comes back to the surface from the depths of lust. Do not ask questions, but go down into the depths of the man who hides his heart and tangled mind," Tombo continued,

"The fire has burned
it has eaten away thoughts
and has not been extinguished."

After a long silence Tombo went on,

"The embers intact
of memory of love
no longer burn.

Here, dead, I live
in the fire of remembrance
and have everything and nothing.

Here, alive, I die
and find what I lose
the self and the mind.

I ask you now
to use your magnifying
glass to see the truth."

Bashu said,

"You cannot have
what it is not, you will have it
if you are no more.

If you want to be
forget to be,
but be here and now.

To penetrate
the senses retreat
and yours is the Way."

Tombo continued,

"The Way appeared
at the thunder of the land
sword on the head.

56

I am by that Way
that leads to you and will go
away from you to me."

He bowed serenely, taking leave of the master. The light in his heart had penetrated into the darkness of the flesh and abandonment of passions, owning up to them without suffering from them. Now he had to catch a glimpse of other ways of casting light on the flesh and the soul.

23. Wrath

"Master, people accuse me of being wrathful. On the contrary, I am as calm as a lake on a windless day. What is wrath?" a young man said to Bashu who, instead of answering, walked straight on. The young man, angered by his indifference, chased him saying, "I have asked you a question. Why do not you answer? Who do you think you are?"

"A stupid question is not worthy of an answer."

"What are you implying? That I am a stupid, perhaps?"

"You have said so," exclaimed Bashu. The young man was hurt by the mockery of his words. His eyes turned red, his face turned purple, his mouth twitched. He worked off his anger on Bashu and heaped fiery words on him, but he remained unmoved by the explosion. Suddenly, the young man struck a blow to his face, which Bashu parried with ease, beating him on the shoulder with a stick, said, "That is what wrath is! It is a calm lake, which surrenders to the wind in an instant, and then flies up into the air."

24. Indignation

"Master, I look around and see a lot of people stricken with grief and suffering many privations. Why do some people say that consciousness, imagination, perception and feelings are empty or illusory? Why do some people say there is no suffering, but there is no absence of suffering, either? Are they blind? Why do some people say that forms, that are continuously changing, are apparent?" a young disciple asked Bashu.

"Why, why, why, it's always 'why' with you," Bashu exclaimed.

"Answer at least one, please" the disciple insisted.

"The last one: If forms are empty, then where something is empty, there is no appearance."

"Master, where something is empty, there is no man. Where there is a man, there is nothing empty. With man come weakness, helplessness, dissatisfaction, and failure. We cannot remain impassive by this," the disciple continued impassioned, "We cannot say that men suffer because they are far from the Way or at the mercy of their passions."

"Yes, we can, because only in this way can we be where we are," replied Bashu.

"I get angry, and I would like to upset the world in an unspeakable rage," the disciple came back.

"Wrath is a dangerous feeling. Passing indignation may be understandable, if you were not here. But you are here. How can you find the Way, if you are angry or indignant?"

"People do not have to tolerate injustice, oppression, and poverty" the disciple replied.

"Your mind reflects on things, but it does not probe into them."

25. Pride

Takarai Kikaku was an educated and intelligent young man. In his free time, he was to be found with his head bent over books for the sake of knowledge. His colleagues were more practical and less intellectual so they left him out of what was going on, they mocked him, they scoffed at his attitudes, and they hid his belongings. In short, they played nasty tricks on him. One day, Takarai went to Bashu and said, "My companions accuse me of being proud, but I was perplexed and incredulous by their allegations. Pride is when you have too high an opinion of yourself, revealed through arrogance or ostentation of talent to the detriment of others. All this is foreign to me. Even denying dependence on illusions and on the gods does not belong to me. Why, then, do they accuse me of pride?"

"Maybe you were not humble enough and this gave rise to resentment," Bashu suggested to the young man.

"No," Takarai answered, "It is just envy because in the discussions I always get the better of them."

"Try not to get the better of them every time. As an American saying goes: The more arguments you win, the less friends you have (Knowles, 2009)."

"No! Why should I give in to an inconclusive argument or mistake so as not to offend those who support it? They treat learning, knowledge of religious doctrine, and the art of dialectic with superiority. They aspire to enlightenment just to enjoy happiness on earth. They are materialists," Takarai concluded with a tone of absolute certainty.

"You look a bit full of yourself, intent on separating and bringing together knowledge and ignorance. Forget what you know in order to remember knowledge. Take part in dialogue but you are wrong to think in terms of absolute truth. Scrutinize your will and you will live the Way," Bashu said to him by way of encouragement.

Takarai Kikaku went away promising to be stronger and more tolerant. The indifference of his companions was sometimes unbearable, not for their jokes, but due to the wall of loneliness that separated him from the others. Takarai, who practised Zen, knew that such incidents would not undermine his imperturbability or alter his self-consciousness. Still, he could not shake off the last of their jokes because for him it seemed like an intolerable humiliation. During their daily cleaning, his schoolfellows had hidden his clothes and he was forced to run naked, overwhelmed by shame.

That night he decided to respond tit-for-tat. In the middle of the night he began shouting, "Fire! Fire!" trying not to be recognized. Everyone was frightened and made a dash for the exit. Finally, they realized it was a joke, but they figured out that it had been him and ridiculed him even more as he had no sense of reality, and he was not able to distinguish between a joke and a serious matter. Takarai suffered the ingratitude of his companions and did not resign himself to the strange and perverse role reversal. He had suffered all their jokes, with or without patience, while they were prepared to take a joke themselves. This difference of treatment bothered him. As soon as the furore died down, everyone went back to sleep. This time Takarai lit a fire for fun, to make the game more real. There was a pall of smoke. Suddenly he repented and tried to put the fire out, but the flames spread rapidly and he lost control of the situation. He began to shout again, "Fire! Fire!" but the schoolfellows paid no attention. Then Bashu ran around among the disciples, bringing down blows with his stick, and pushed them out quickly. The premises were completely destroyed, despite strenuous efforts to put the fire out.

In the end, they sat down, all of them tired. Takarai stood up, his head bowed, and ready to take the punishment that he deserved and expressing a wish to go away after expiating his guilt. Bashu said, "This, surely, is pride." Takarai begged for forgiveness and bowed down, crying like a baby. Bashu called on the others to express their views. They all agreed he had to be driven out with shame. Bashu said, "We need someone to help us rebuild." They were all amazed by his indulgence. They expected Takarai to be beaten and punished. Instead, here was Bashu talking about the need for labour. They would work harder and Takarai could go somewhere else to study his books, reflecting on being and nothingness. Takarai's face was streaked with tears but without a groan or a grimace. He knew what they thought and he felt the hardness of their hearts against him. There was a long silence amid the acrid and nauseating smell of burning. No one dared to speak any more. Bashu began, saying, "You made fun of Takarai, but he didn't learn anything from it. Indeed, he was trapped in the labyrinth of the mind. If he goes away, who will teach him to get out of the labyrinth? If he goes away, how will he expiate his guilt and learn the humility that comes with true forgiveness?"

The disciples were speechless but they agreed with Bashu's decision and no longer urged him to send the culprit away. Takarai stayed, and dedicated his time to the reconstruction and meditation. His body was tired, but his mind was alert as he laboured over the stones and the planks of wood. The house was rebuilt. His ideas faded into the background as he worked in the kitchen or in the paddy field. His head became lighter as he dug the hard ground, while knowledge and the pleasure of knowledge faded away, ignoring the tradition of his fathers: no mind, no thought, no logic, no will, no body. The sense of denial permeated his thoughts and actions. The truth emerged from sowing and reaping grain, cooking and washing dishes, meditating and sleeping. He did not repress the consciousness of knowledge and even indulged his longing to study. His talk was empty and it did not lead anywhere: Right and wrong were mixed up in an endless stream of propositions. His books conveyed knowledge without vitality, because they were embedded in the past and without the possibility of repeating the same as before. Meditating in silence remained the only option.

One cold November day he was meditating in the garden. Suddenly, his eyes were attracted by the golden petals of a chrysanthemum. Faced with such splendour, he was aware of the darkness of his mind that was breathtaking. Life and death were conjoined at the breaking point of the unity of spirit and matter, and humility pervaded his heart, leaving a vacuum. He was happy and ecstatic, as his entire world and being were concentrated in that moment of complete reversal of the order of things. He fainted. After a while he came to his senses and returned to his room, where he described what had happened.

A chrysanthemum
gives light and there is no sun
I bow and I am

Grain of earth
that burns nourishing petals
of light in the void.

The experience was indescribable, and could only communicate from heart to heart, from soul to soul. The doors of thunder opened up. Tremors broke out in his body and mind. The resistance of the dark was shattered in a flash of joy. He experienced an unexpected awakening, and went to Bashu. Now he felt no shame for his past, no concern for his status. He was serene. Bashu was there to welcome him like the water of the lake or the wings of a fowl. Bashu looked at him and invited him to come closer. He approached a little in response to this gesture, but Bashu urged him to come even closer. He reached out to touch his feet and to stroke his face. Then Bashu said, after an interminable silence, "I cannot say in words, but you can go now because the corn is ripe and the reaper as well. Your place is in you, no more here." Takarai bowed in gratitude for his salvation by the skin of his teeth, but there was no debt of love because it was free of charge. His being in that state was the best gift for his master.

26. Sloth

"If to act is not to act, why do we not idle away our time from morning till night, delighting in doing nothing?" a monk asked Bashu defiantly.

"Doing nothing is doing everything" and, for the avoidance of doubt, Bashu added, "Not doing anything means just following the natural flow of things."

"Well, Master, then why do we need to sow the seed and then pick the fruits?" the monk continued firmly.

"It is not you that sows the seed, but it is the seed that sows you. It is not you that picks the fruit, but it is the fruit that picks you."

"That may be," the monk said, puzzled. "But not to act is to do nothing, to be idle. There are many people who suffer humiliating failures. I would like to dedicate myself to helping the needy."

"Follow your inclination and feel free," Bashu replied.

At lunchtime, an empty bowl was placed before the monk. He complained to the *tenzo*, the cook, about the way he was being treated. Bashu intervened in the dispute and said, "Why do you toil to eat?" The monk was offended at these words and withdrew to his room, where he stayed without leaving on any account. After the third day, Bashu went to see him and said, "You are slothful because you are proud. In fact, you believe neither in what you say, nor in what you do."

"No. I really believe in what I say," the monk replied in a flash. "Meditation is a useless activity."

"Why, then, are you locked up here with your thoughts? Do you see that oak tree?"

"Yes, I see it."

"Does it move?"

"No, it doesn't! At the very least, you cannot see it."

"In its immobility it is active. Truly, I say to you that there is nothing as active as that oak tree."

27. Sloth, meditation, and conscience

"The practice of meditation means you sit down, calm, motionless, with your mind perfectly empty. Sometimes, I wonder what is the sense of sitting or standing there like a caryatid. At other times, I sink into absolute sloth like inert matter. What is the meaning of all this?"

"The meaning of sloth or inertia, if you like this term."

"I wanted to say that you need to overcome the state of acquiescence that undermines practice and drowsy consciousness," the monk continued.

"It is not practice that makes the conscience sleepy, but consciousness that makes practice sleepy," Bashu pressed him.

"Master, I thought you could achieve that after a period of contemplation in the countryside following the steps of the soul. I know that sitting or standing motionless is a kind of a perfect movement without apparent motion, and that a void is not nothingness, but it is emptiness filled with knowledge that makes you a living being because conscience affects practice."

"Even practice affects conscience," Bashu remarked.

"These are the words," said the monk. "I feel outside of talk and feel only indolence."

"If you think and talk, you are not thinking. If you talk and think about it, you are not talking. What do you do? Speak! Speak!" Bashu pressed him, interrupting him.

"Master, how can I talk, if I do not think?"

"So, think without talking" said Bashu dismissing him.

28. The avarice of feelings

"Father, I am going to a monastery," Nakamura's eldest son said to him. Nakamura, surprised and displeased, answered, "Let your will be done, and may you find happiness." With feigned disinterest, he added, "You will not be here at home anymore, and the emptiness following your departure will never be filled, but I cannot change your intentions."

"Why do you say that, father?" The son said. "You are selfish. You have always thought about yourself for as long as I have known you, you see only yourself, and you love only yourself. You are a miser. Ah! Finally, I have said it! And so I have freed myself," the son concluded with an acrimonious tone. He threw off his cloak, took off his shoes and went out of the house.

The father was stunned and did not say a word. For less serious matters, he had beaten his son many times in the past. Now, he was meditating on those words like an idiot. Was he selfish? He did not know! He had always thought only of his family. First of all he thought of his parents and then of his wife and his children. If this attitude was selfish, he did not understand anything, and still less did he deserve anything. He was stunned and did not say a word. The worm had become lodged in his mind that was now devoid of thoughts, increasing a flow of emotions, reflections, questions, and changes of heart. There was a void in his consciousness that destabilized him. There was a tear that could not mend. He did not say a word, but was lost in thought. Was he, perhaps, too detached from his nearest and dearest? Was he too detached from what was going on around him? Had he shown little interest in the events that had taken place and in which he was the protagonist? Maybe that was indeed the case. He had taken care of others but not of himself, and the focus was not always aimed at intimate introspection. His activity had absorbed him so much that he tended to forget his bodily needs. He had thought of others, not of himself. Then, he thought about nothing and no one.

Nakamura fell into a state of absolute prostration. He could not work anymore, he could not sleep and he could not eat. His absent-mindedness and apathy worried his wife who begged him to retreat for a time to a monastery to meditate. This might have helped him. In that state, he was not able to do any of his usual work. His wife had to take over his duties, aided only by her two daughters. Nakamura took his leave and went to a monastery, but not the same one as his son. He was placed among the novices and began the practice of meditation. Slowly, his thoughts subsided and peace took hold of his mind. The state of emotional anaesthesia was still his shadow, but his sorrow was the avarice which prevented him from understanding anything. He did not want comfort, wealth, worldly goods, fame or power. Yet, he felt that his avarice was a cause of concern. So one day he went to Bashu, he described his problem and ended by saying, "Master, can a man be greedy and at the same time feel the need to give to others?"

"There is giving which is prodigality, and there is giving which is avarice," Bashu said to him.

"This means I could have an attitude that has prevented my giving?" he asked thoughtfully, almost to himself. After a brief pause, Nakamura added, "It could be, but I have always given freely and in a disinterested manner. How can I have given rise to feelings of resentment or detachment?"

"There is a donor and a beneficiary. Equal exchange can only take place if the beneficiary is on the same wavelength as the donor."

"Well, was I not attentive to the people to whom I gave or who were around me?" Nakamura asked, surprised and disappointed.

"Maybe. You have not told me anything about yourself, but only about your own actions. There is avarice and avarice. The avarice of feelings is no less serious than the

avarice of material goods," Bashu answered, dismissing him
with a nod.

29. The avarice of things

In the village everyone knew that Kado Tota had amassed his wealth by taking advantage of every opportunity and exploiting his workers in an unscrupulous manner. He was not touched even in the face of dying beggars and at times even recruited workers from among them. Those who knocked on his door to get a loaf of bread received as offer to work all day to be fed, and were often sent away after receiving a portion of food that was totally insufficient. Once he was summoned to court because even a beggar demanded a decent wage, but his defence was impeccable, "Your Honour, the plaintiff, who is here before you, knocked on my door asking for something to eat. I suggested doing some work in the rice fields to earn it. He accepted the proposal, and I kept my word. I do not understand why he asks for more. I gave him just what he asked, that is, something to eat, and this was what we agreed on."

"Your Honour," interrupted the beggar. "It is not true. He is telling lies."

"Excuse me!" replied Kado. "Didn't I bring you a bowl of rice on the job?"

"Yes," admitted the beggar. "But I was still hungry."

"You did the work of one man, why did you want to eat for two?" Kado replied. The judge ruled in favour of Kado, and the poor man was beaten because he had no money to pay the costs of the case. Then he was released. In the village, all the workers feared Kado's reaction and accepted their employment conditions without any individual bargaining. He owned all the farmland, wells, and springs in the area. All the villagers depended on his needs, because without his patronage, they would have starved.

Kado was feared even in the family. No-one could say a word or ask for anything with impunity. Each request was systematically turned down and the rare concessions were reduced to the essentials. His response was always the same. "You sucked the lifeblood out of me: Vampires, leeches, freeloaders, loafers, spendthrifts of my savings. You are spongers, greedy for my wealth." In truth, when someone came forward with a request, he immediately became agitated, as if they had asked him to cut off his hand. Kado clammed up and attacked them.

One year there was a drought and famine that affected the villagers. The disciples of Bashu undertook to seek aid from distant villages not affected by drought. They went from house to house to help families in need. During a tour, Bashu met Kado and Kado insulted him. "Slacker, where are you going?"

"Are you talking about yourself?" Bashu said.

"No, I am talking about you," Kado shot back.

"Ah, yes? I see you do not look at yourself. The only slacker in the village is you," Bashu replied firmly.

"Ignorant! Arrogant! You are talking about something you don't know about. Let me tell you that I think day and night about how to earn what I have earned! I am always busy."

"Taking care of your assets," Bashu interrupted him.

"Why shouldn't I? Is that so bad? The others want to get their hands on my assets without having to work, like birds of prey, carnivores and robbers."

"If there is someone who does not work here, that is you," Bashu said. The calm of Bashu destroyed Kado, who began to shout insults, "Worm. Beggar. You are an insolent fellow if ever there was one! Do you live by the sweat of your brow? Do you work? You should be in jail. How dare you judge me!"

"I do not judge, I see," Bashu said and walked away, while Kado barked out more insults and became angrier and angrier. The fact of being ignored irritated him to the point that he decided to run after him with a view to beating him. Kado attacked Bashu from behind, but Bashu spun around and parried the blow, disarming him with a clever move and throwing his stick away. Kado could not believe his eyes. That insignificant monk had dared to rebel against him, the presumptuous parasite had dared to humiliate him. It could not end like this. Kado attacked him with his bare hands, but he lost his balance due to a move by Bashu and fell to the ground. Bashu walked away undisturbed, with Kado yelling in the dust. He screamed and did not get up. He was shocked. His belligerence did not allow him to stand up. After a while, he hoisted himself on his spindly legs and headed home, slowly and with a grim expression on his face, more vicious than ever. He felt alone and separate from the others. He turned his thoughts over and over in his mind and realized that he was not interested in others because he was satisfied with what he had and what he was. He only had the pleasure of contemplating his land and riches.

Suddenly he realized that things were not as before. Trouble came so suddenly and caught him unprepared. He was overtaken by melancholy and nostalgia. It was not possible that this had happened to him. He had everything now and enjoyed it. Now an imperceptible veil of mist came between him and the things he possessed, a thin layer that made complete and total possession impossible. He might get sick. He might die and lose what he had acquired over time. He would be at the mercy of others. What was this wall between him and the world? He felt divided, isolated, detached, and separate from the things he possessed. He did not give in to these sensations. He reacted with determination and turned to his possessions, his gold and his crops, breathing a sigh of relief, albeit only temporary.

A few years later he fell ill and could barely speak, but cursed the world with gestures and grunts. He knew the end was near, so he called for Bashu, who arrived as soon as he could, but when he got there, Kado spoke no more. His gaze met that of Bashu and nobody could make out what passed in the eyes of Kado: perhaps a spark of life that resisted and survived to the end. Bashu bowed, approached him and hugged him tenderly. After a while, he turned to Kado's wife and two children, to give them courage. Kado was no more, and nobody will ever know if he repented or was lost among the things he loved. For the covetous there is no gratitude, but compassion is for everyone. Only Bashu perhaps knew, but it did not make sense to talk about it. What was gone was gone. Svaha!

30. Gluttony

Sawaki Suzuko could not resist the temptation of tidbits and delicacies. Even when he was full, he went crazy for delicacies and stole them from the larder, using any trick to devour them. Sawaki had become skilful at pilfering anything under the eyes of the onlookers. Nevertheless, every now and then they discovered him, and sometimes punished him severely. One day he slipped into the kitchens of the local landowner and drank and ate in abundance. He managed to shake off the servants when he was discovered, but he was recognized and had to flee the country because the local landowner could not suffer such behaviour on the part of anyone. He would not be able to endure the punishment that would have been inflicted on him by law. He would not be a coward. He had always paid for his misdeeds with his head held high, every time he had been discovered. Now he fled to avoid the corporal punishment for this crime, but he also wanted to avoid falling into temptation. He had taken an irrevocable decision: He would retire to a monastery to practise meditation because he did not want to be the victim of his gluttony. He went to Bashu and asked him to be accepted. Bashu agreed, provided that Sawaki was willing to work in the kitchen.

"Master," Sawaki begged, "how can I work well when temptation will get the better of me every time? Please, assign me to another task: washing the pots and floors, digging the fields, chopping wood, pruning trees, digging ditches, fasting. I cannot come into contact with food. Resisting temptation would be a torture. I would die of temptation."

"Now, are you alive or dead?"

"I don't know." Then, he went on. "Neither one nor the other. I am one and the other. I am nothing and I am everything." Faced with the silence of Bashu, he pleaded for mercy, "Give me an alternative, please."

"Go to work in the kitchen, or go back to the village to pay off your debt," Bashu insisted.

"I am afraid I will fail. Help me."

"You are stronger than you think," Bashu encouraged him.

Sawaki Suzuko bowed and thanked the master. Then he went to perform his duties. He resisted temptation for a long time. One day he gave in, and stole some fruit from the pantry. It was not a large amount, but as he had broken his vow, he started to steal again and again. After a few months the shortages could not be hidden anymore. One day during lunch, the person in charge asked those present to tell him who had stolen from the pantry. Everyone stood up, except Sawaki, and said, "It was me." Moved by such generosity, Sawaki burst into tears and went to hide away in the corner. He sat meditating and did not move. After three days, the disciples came to Bashu, begging him to go to Sawaki to convince him to break his fast because they had been asked him to do so, but he had refused. Bashu arrived, entered, bowed, and said, "Enjoy your meal."

"My appetite is good, maybe too good, but after eating my appetite is the same as before. To eat and to fast are just a reflection of the emptiness of life. I am empty and a failure," Sawaki said with pride and boldness. Bashu remained silent. After a long pause, Sawaki began to speak but Bashu interrupted him, saying, "That which is empty is full, and that which is full is empty, so you don't need to eat."

"In fact, as you see, I am not eating. Yesterday I was hungry and ate something, now no more," he replied as if wishing to excuse himself. The master spoke patiently, "That which is empty exists because there is that which is full. Your emptiness should be filled so that you become empty again."

"That which is full is for those who are worthy. I am unworthy. I wish to stay empty," Sawaki replied feebly.

76

"You are free to do as you wish, but your friends have an empty stomach and are waiting for the fruits of your labour. Back to the kitchen," Bashu ordered him. The voice of the teacher struck a blow to his heart and Sawaki broke down in tears, even though he had said nothing special.

"I am not able to control myself," Sawaki added, sobbing. "I cannot stand in the kitchen, in the eye of temptation."

"Wrong. If you are able to fast, you are able to refrain from stealing food. You do not know about the longing for food. You do not know the nature of food. You want food to become part of you, so that you own it, but life is already in you, and you stifle life because you are afraid to live. Go back to cooking food. Try to bring out the vitality of the food and enrich it with your vitality transferred. Be food for the food and condiment for condiment."

Sawaki returned to the kitchen hesitantly, but determined to follow the advice of the master, to enter the soul of food, to discover flavours and properties, to follow his inner voice. Gradually, he found himself immersed in his work and his gestures were integrated with the end product: from the collection of food to cutting, from the cooking it to carrying it to the table. Each action or element had a role in exalting flavours, aromas, and energy. He cooked tirelessly, experimenting with the best combinations of ingredients in accordance with the nature of the food. One day Bashu came in and, instead of greeting him, as always, struck him on the shoulder with the Keisaku. Sawaki, who was savouring a dish, was stunned. He recovered after a while and meditated for a long time. He realized that he had been freed from his obsessions. A great joy came over him. He went to the master with fear and impatience, to tell the tale.

"Hunger was filled
by the satisfied senses
but hunger remains.

The food is in me:
a blow dealt on my shoulder
has revealed that.

Full and emptiness
filled each other
satiated with food."

Bashu said,

"Not by food alone
do you feed yourself, but by virtue
where there is no more.

The end is not
the end, but the beginning
of returning to self."

Bashu dismissed him with another blow. Sawaki bowed low, and with a broad smile returned to the kitchen to prepare lunch for everyone. It was to be the beginning of a long journey.

31. Finding sense

Kuroda, a young woman studying Zen Buddhism, asked Bashu. "Enlightenment is not dependent on the mind, why then should we meditate or study? It does not depend on the body, why then should we remain seated until we are at the end of our strength, practising the harsh discipline of the body? It is not a matter of chance, why then is the experience enhanced by chance, which illuminates it? It leaves nothing, total emptiness, even if it is not nothing or emptiness. It happens by chance. Given the uncertainty of its occurrence, why should we aspire to *satori* and strive so much to achieve it, when it comes alone and in unexpected ways?"

"Why should we be born if we have to die? Why should we breathe in, if we have to breathe out? Why should we waste our breath speaking, if we can keep quiet?"

"Master, I want to find the sense in acting and thinking. I get lost in trying to find the truth that is elusive. The depth of our origins lies in the mind, phenomena are changing incessantly, and reality exists as a reflection of thought. I have a perception that everything is an illusion. The body is an illusion, my ideas are illusions, illusion is the ground that I tread on, illusion is the water that quenches my thirst, and illusion is the air that I breathe."

"Try not to breathe," Bashu interrupted her.

"I cannot do it. Yes, I could do it, but then I would die and move to another state, continuing to live on the ground that I trod on and in the air that I breathed, in the perpetual cycle of forms. Master, the plane that separates things is a virtual image.

Flight of the sparrow
on water where it is reflected
and at that moment it changes.

It is the self, forehand and backhand.
Slight breath of wind
and on water there is no more."

"Are you that sparrow?" Bashu asked.

"Yes, I am that sparrow and I am afraid of not succeeding: in overcoming the duality of beings divided between being there and not being there, in revealing the shadows of what separates us from the truth, in overcoming the contradictory nature of existence. I feel the need to look for that *je ne sais quoi* (enlightenment) that I cannot find. I feel the need to run away."

"You do not need to escape, nor to try," Bashu replied.

"I will commit myself without commitment, ready to lose everything to find everything. But why is this not enough to recover the unity in the multiplicity of sensations and emotions?"

"If you do not find the right way, you will not get out of the maze. Here is a way forward: Forget about feelings and emotions aimed at achieving the union of each single element with the whole."

Overcome with emotion Kuroda responded to the master with the following lines,

"The peach tree is bare
then it blossoms and has leaves
it has fruits and loses its leaves.

It is one and many
I am the peach-stone taken away
to the fallow land."

He replied,

"You cultivate so much
that the buried peach-stone
will be a tall plant."

Then, Bashu dismissed her and when she bowed, he brought down a gentle blow with the Keisaku, between her shoulder and neck. With an innocent smile she turned round and went away, light in her flight like a sparrow in the dawn breeze.

32. Empty thoughts

A novice said to Bashu, "We get up at three or four in the morning and recite sutras. Then, we put on the kesa and we practice zazen[12] until seven o'clock, breakfast time. After reciting more sutras, we remain silent until nine o'clock. Then we practise zazen until eleven. We rest until twelve, lunch time, and remain in absolute silence. After lunch, we attend the teacher's lessons and from three to five o'clock in the afternoon we practise zazen again. From five to seven o'clock we carry out our ablutions. From seven to nine o'clock, we practise zazen. Finally, we retire to bed. This is a life far removed from real life, where men suffer and work hard to get food. Here everything is prepared, served without charge, and we think only of meditation. It is a convenient life, but it is a useless life."

"Sometimes, we need something useless," Bashu replied humbly.

"It is not only unnecessary, it is empty and meaningless," the novice argued.

"Many people believe they are full and actually they are empty. Where there is a void, there is also a vessel that is full because nothing can harm it, but they do not know. However, many thoughts fill the self, obscuring our true essence to see the state that lies beyond. Perhaps, the true essence is buried by vain desire or presumptuousness."

"Are you insinuating that I am a presumptuous?"

"Those are your words not mine."

---

[12] Zazen is the core of the Zen Buddhist practice aimed at remaining seated, that is, suspending all judgmental thinking and letting words, ideas, images, thoughts pass by without being involved in them.

33. Words and silence

A layman asked Bashu, "Language expresses distinctions and differences to reflect a changing and complex reality, to represent nuances and moods. Words, which are the elements of language, derive from a process of abstraction that lacks the reality of its authenticity. I wonder how we can communicate without words, without these in misleading limitations, without the impossibility of being in intimate contact with others through the truth. Am I right? What are words?" Bashu remained impassive and silent.

"Please, give me an answer, a sign," implored the layman.

"Kwatz"[13] Bashu shouted, with a powerful and visceral tone that frightened the man. After recovering, however, he continued undeterred. "Words are true and false, real and fictitious. After words have been spoken, there is no longer any meaning, nor the ego that communicated it." Bashu had written something in the dust with his stick, while the layman spoke. Then he struck his stick three times on the ground drawing attention to what he had written, and while the layman was intent on reading, Bashu struck him, suddenly, with a resounding blow with his stick on the neck, dismissing him. "Words are the obsession of silence. Think more and speak less."

---

[13] Kwatz is the word the Zen master shouts to the distracted pupil to urge him to greater concentration. The scream starts from hara (Deshimaru, 1977a, p. 89/192). Hara refers to the intestines from an anatomical point of view, while it indicates the concentration of important nerves from the physiological point of view. It is a centre of energy and activity, which becomes vigorous with the practice of zazen and proper breathing.

34. Freedom

A disciple asked Bashu, "Teacher, what is freedom?"

"To do what you feel comfortable doing: To drink when you are thirsty, eat when you are hungry, and sleep when you are tired."

"This is freedom of action, but I mean also freedom of thought, and thus of protest."

"Where there is thought, there is action. Where there is no action, there is no thought," Bashu objected.

"It is not true! There is a reflex action that shows action without thought. There is an abstract logical reasoning that does not imply any action. Although from a certain perspective, thoughts and actions always coexist, freedom is not embedded in them. If I think I am free, I risk being in prison without knowing it. What sense do drinking, eating, and sleeping have when a powerful leader could limit our freedom and even our chance to think?"

"I have not seen any powerful figure, who has assured them" Bashu said drily.

"For me, freedom means allowing everyone to be and realize the Self," he said with pride, and continued, "Freedom means acting and thinking according to your feelings. Kings, dictators, and powerful leaders may have ensured their subjects can drink and eat ..." But before finishing the sentence, he received a blow from Bashu with a stick and was sent away.

The disciple meditated all night. The next day he came back to Bashu and said, "Teacher, I meditated and I understood. Freedom means drinking when you are thirsty, eating ..."

"No," Bashu interrupted him abruptly. "Freedom means acting and thinking according to your true feelings."

"Well!" he said with a puzzled expression on his face. "Master, yesterday, I said that too ...", but he could not finish the phrase, because Bashu took his breath away with another blow and sent him back to his real occupation. The disciple worked hard but he was angry. The sweat streamed down his forehead. The more he worked, the more his thoughts ran away from him. He felt light, like a thread of a cobweb in the wind, a feather in the upward motion of the air, a hollow bamboo cane. The lightness emptied him. The more he emptied, the more he filled up with nothing. The more he suffered the yoke of rules, the more he felt free. He worked and meditated. He meditated and worked. The body was changed by work and meditation. The changes of his body influenced his thought. The changes of his thought influenced his body.

One morning he got up and saw that he could not think any more, he was empty. He was inert and vibrating in the natural flow of feelings, which emerged from the core of a strong and disciplined body. He dug in the fresh air. Between his sweat and the smell of the earth, a thought occurred to him, "Freedom is work." Everything he had thought now seemed dull and meaningless. His beliefs seemed silly. The world appeared in a different light. It was too easy! Freedom was not to receive instructions, not to be tied down, not to have obligations. Freedom was the whole body of things, which guaranteed the practice of the individual. Freedom was experience!

I dig the earth
and gather berries
free and in peace.

I chop firewood
and in the sky I mirror
alone and satisfied.

A butterfly
on the cherry blossom
detaches a petal.

The heron dances
in the air and its wings play
pranks on the clouds.

The butterfly and heron
chase each other in the air
a dance of nothing.

He savoured his serenity. Now he knew the truth as his mind subsided from the minutiae of nothing and all the events presented themselves in a different and inexplicable light, granting him a sense of fullness. He picked up a handful of damp earth in his left hand and went to Bashu. He greeted, smiled, opened his hand, then he clenched it hard and brought it to his chest. Bashu smiled. The disciple bowed and walked away without a word.

35. Living is wishing

"Man is alive if he wants something, if he is pervaded by the instinct to do, to be. But we need to tame our passions. We anaesthetize them because when our desires are unfulfilled, they cause frustration and sorrow. We flee from life to escape pain. Is this right, Master?" a disciple said to Bashu, who responded immediately with a blow with his stick. The disciple looked at him with puzzled eyes. In response to his dismay, Bashu cried aloud, "If you flee from me to escape from pain, you flee from life. If you do not flee from me not to flee from pain, you escape from life. Now what do you do? Tell me, what do you do?"

"Master, I asked for a response, not for a riddle," he replied hard-nosed and continued, "A life detached from the world does not involve us in the suffering of being. Maybe it isolates us from pain; but is this living? Living means being immersed in desire, and desire means suffering for what you do not get, and suffering is living. Do we want to be without life?"

"Are you without life?" Bashu interrupted him.

"No," he admitted candidly. "However, the meditation leads us away from the essence of daily survival, where there is suffering, to the realm of contemplation, where there is ataraxia, that means serene calmness."

"Even our discipline involves suffering," Bashu interrupted again and with a wide sweep of the arm he dismissed him.

36. Anxiety

A disciple asked Bashu, "Teacher, I am often assailed by a sense of unreasonable anxiety, which whistles like a lashing wind in my ears. My whole body is in the throes of an uncontrollable force. Behind my neck there is a sharp razor, in front of my face there is a burning flame. I think of life and cannot find my way any more. I think about death and feel a sense of desperate futility. Nothing and everything is blurry. The scent of life intoxicates my mind and the stench of death cools my heart. The spider's web exhausts my strength and the predator comes upon me in a threatening way. Is this anxiety?"

"Those words are yours," Bashu answered.

"I said it, but I do not know whether it is so, so I ask someone else. For example, I ask Bashu. What is the sense of living in the emptiness of existence? What is the sense of indifference that permeates the relations of men, who seek genuine friendship? What is the sense of this rift between the self and others? What is this lump in my throat? It does not go up, it does not go down, and it burns my windpipe. Why is it that the more you seek happiness, the more you dig a ditch around you?"

Bashu interrupted him, "Why this yearning to understand who you are? Why do you not give yourself up to the impossibility of being what you hope to be? Why do you want to join others, when you cannot join yourself? Please, answer. Tell me something."

"You have to tell me! If not, why would I have asked you that question?" the disciple said from the bottom of his heart.

"The answers are within you and it is up to you to discover them." In silence, Bashu took him by the arm, and led him into the garden, and sat down near the pond. After a while, a fly darted across the water, tracing intricate swirls in the clear air. Suddenly a trout jumped out of the water and caught the fly before plunging down below the surface. The master pulled his ear sharply, pinching it and making him scream, then got up and slipped away like a ghost, leaving him facing the dilemma of life and death.

The next day Bashu met him and said, "Let us go to see the pond."

The disciple replied, "Yesterday I did not hear. Today, I hear very well."

37. The sound of hands

The young Tanno came to see Bashu asking him for training in the solution of koans. However, he was given instructions to take the firewood to the kitchen and clean the pots. At the end of a year of hard work, he returned to Bashu begging him to instruct him in Zen. The ardour of the young led Bashu to accept. He suggested showing the sound of one hand clapping.

Tanno meditated for three days and finally came to Bashu and said, "The sound of one hand clapping is an impossible sound because you cannot produce it using only one hand."

"If it was impossible, I would have not asked it. This is not your answer, but one of the books that you have read. I want to hear only your own! Go back and meditate," he replied and sent him away.

Tanno was puzzled. He gave the right answer, but it was not accepted. Why? What was the mystery of the sound of one hand clapping? Nothing. It was pure nonsense to harass the innocent for no reason. In any case, two hands were not clapping. In the worst case, they cheered or made a thunderous noise. He went back to meditate, despite these burning doubts, lost completely in his thoughts. He forgot all his material needs. After three days of total isolation, he returned to Bashu and said, "I have found it. The sound of one hand is this." He raised his right hand to his chest's height and began to snap his fingers on the palm of the same hand. Soft clapping was heard in the silence of the room.

"That is the sound of your fingers on your palm, not the sound of one hand clapping," Bashu said.

"The sound of one hand is opposed to that of two hands. If I clap two hands, the fingers of one fall on the palm of the other. It follows that to tap the fingers on the palm of the hand to which they belong is the sound of one hand."

"Not necessarily," said Bashu.

"So, let me hear the sound of two hands," cried Tanno impatiently. Bashu spread his hands on his chest and knocked hard on the cheeks of Tanno, who was so irritated by this that he kicked out at the shin of Bashu, without hitting it because the blow was deftly avoided.

"Ah," Bashu cried, "That is the best you can do. Go back to carrying the firewood into the kitchen and meditating on the sound of one hand clapping. Go, you slacker."

"What can I do?" Tanno cried with remorse for his rebellious action and for fear of getting lost.

"The question should become a hot coal in your shoes. You cannot take it away, because the land on which you tread is buried under fire. You will burn if you stop longer than the time required to take your steps. Only in this way, the koan becomes the embers of truth on your steps, it turns into a hot liquid which you gulp down to burn what remains of conventional thinking."

"When will I know that I have found the right answer?"

"You will know all on your own. Come on, go! Go back to washing the pots." Tanno turned slowly towards the kitchen, but he suspected he had taken a step forward while going backward.

38. The Christian monk

A Christian monk, Katsumura Okano, presented himself to Bashu and said, "Master, I beg you to count me among your disciples."

"Aaah! How can you call me master?" Bashu replied with mock surprise. "You should address another One only with this title."

"Please! Spare me your sarcasm. If you are a teacher, you are also a master. If you teach me, you will be my master."

"That may be so for teaching, but you are lying, and you are aware of the fact. What can I teach you that you don't know already? Then you have the courage to say you are my disciple. Come on! You already have a master whose disciple you are. Go back where you came from. You have come to the wrong monastery," Bashu concluded, returning to his room and closing the door behind him. Katsumura Okano did not give up easily. As a result, he did not lose heart. He settled down in a secluded corner waiting for the next time. In the evening, the disciples took pity on him and invited him to eat with them, but he refused, only expressing a wish to remain. Diligent and loving, they brought him a blanket for the night. In the morning, when Bashu came by, Okano greeted him and told him he was going to ignore his advice. He pleaded, "Please! Teach me Zen."

"If you learn, you will be empty. If you don't learn, you will be empty anyway. Zen is of no great use to you. Go back to your monastery," Bashu insisted.

"If I learn emptiness, I can be full. Then, having learned what is not of great use to me, it will have been of use at least to the glory of my God," Okano said.

"The glory of your God is already great, with or without Zen."

"It is true, and the glory of my God is also mine."

"You have it already and you cannot look for what you already have, you cannot learn what you already know, you cannot try to be what you should already be," Bashu said patiently.

"What I am, I am, but I understand only what I am learning (or going through). What I know is everything and nothing, what I do not know is just everything," Okano said with conviction.

"From your petulance it is clear that your religion does not know humility, or you have not learned it yet," Bashu concluded and went away. Katsumura Okano stayed there, still and concentrating on nothing. Also that day he turned down the invitation to have dinner with the disciples, and drank only tea. The next morning, a novice said to him, "How can you believe in Christ and Buddha?"

"Why? Do you believe in Buddha?" Okano said. "If you believe you are lost! And if you do not believe you are lost all the same. Come on! Tell me, what do you do? Hurry up! Reply." The novice was confused. Disappointed, he walked away under the eyes of Bashu, who had just arrived. Then Bashu said to Okano, "I see that you are complicated, perhaps you have forgotten that blessed are those of a gentle spirit: They shall inherit the earth and the kingdom of heaven shall be theirs. You afflict us with your perseverance, but it was written: Blessed are those who are sorrowful, they shall find consolation. Will you, then, still remain to magnify our affliction?" (Matthew 5.3-10).

"Yes," Okano replied proudly and continued. "You will not discourage me with your provocations. Please teach me Zen. There is no contradiction between Zen and Christianity. My faith cannot be an obstacle to knowledge."

"I cannot teach you what you already know," Bashu said drily.

"I am not asking you to teach me the word of God or of Buddha, but only meditation," Okano objected.

"In a house where you have removed the walls and floors, where will you put all the furnishings? How can you follow the path of Zen without going the way indicated by Buddha? How can you sit in meditation, without training to be a sitting Buddha? Will you think you are a seated Christ?" Bashu replied, mocking and irreverent.

"Why do you speak so harshly? I am not put off by your mockery because I am determined to learn. I wish to seek the truth where it is. I wish to understand the nature of the human mind, which is not for the exclusive use of Buddhism," Okano said almost to himself, with a mournful air.

"And if the truth were other than your God?" Bashu replied.

"Where the truth is, there is also God, necessarily. If Zen is the Truth, then God is there too," and, after uttering these words, he grimaced in repentance, as his words seemed to be blasphemous.

"Zen is not the means to know the Way, but the Way itself. Are you ready to give up everything?" Bashu asked, trying not to hurt him.

"Oh! God, forgive me," he said, raising his eyes to heaven, and continued, turning to Bashu. "I have given up everything for Him. What do I still have to give up?"

"Lo and behold, you are already on the Way, with the Truth, in the Light. What more are you looking for?"

"I am looking for the unity of body and mind that I cannot achieve with my own faith. Perhaps, the faith that I have is not ideal but I cultivate it as best I can."

"Does not the faith you have in Christ, that springs from your heart, pervade your mind? Is not the harmony of the circularity of the heart and mind the true nature of man you are looking for? Does not the union of man with the world come from the love of Christ? Reflect on this. You insist on finding what should be or is already in you."

"Oh! Thank you, Master! Your words are like light in the darkness. My faith is in the word of Christ; but I have experience of this union in the mind, not in my body. I conceive it in the afterlife, not in the earthly life. It is a limitation of mine that I wish to overcome and you can help me, I know! Love, which is the essence of the Word, does not live only in faith, but in a rigorous and intense spirit of sacrifice and dedication. It is not the word that makes you for Christ, but your being that makes your word for Christ. By means of meditation, I try to be a crucified Christ, rather than a seated Buddha," he dared to reply.

"You experience faith even with the body. I think you are guilty of the sin of presumption or you have some eccentric ideas or a misplaced faith. I don't think He wants it. He was crucified for you. Your place is not here. Goodbye!" Bashu concluded and went away.

Okano was humiliated and angry with himself. He was unable to find an answer and was completely lost in the pain of rejection, in the network of words. Then he curled up, resting his forehead between his crossed legs and sat there for so long that he lost track of time and became stiff. He felt like a turtle-shell, ossified, calcified, drained, crushed, bruised, and battered. The world seemed to focus on the line formed from his forehead and, following the contour of the chest and belly, joined with his chin. Suddenly he came to his senses and became aware of the environment, but did not have the strength to change position and remained still. He did not know how long he had been there, but he knew that Bashu would be coming and he would be aware of his presence without looking around. As it happened, Okano greeted Bashu before they came near him, imploring him, "Master, give me any tasks and, please, allow me into the dojo! Give me your Dokusans."[14]

---

[14] Dojo (bodhimanda in Sanskrit) is the formal training place where disciples practise Zen meditation and conduct examinations and other related encounters. In fact, it results from Do (Tao), which indicates the "Way", and Jo, which indicates that "place". Therefore, it is the "hall of the Way": The place reserved for the practice of different training disciplines, including zazen and some martial arts. The term zendo is preferably used for zazen. The Dokusan refers to a private personal interview or meeting between a Zen student and the master: It is an opportunity for the student to

"No doubt about it. When one says tenacity, you are a living example. Let us proceed with the experiment. You can choose between the vegetable garden and the kitchen."

"I choose the care of the garden," Okano said.

"I knew it," Bashu said and went away.

Okano devoted himself entirely to Zen (meditation) and the care of the garden. Meditation predisposed him to get in touch with his body. He trained it to be there, where it was, at that very moment with his entire self. His work in the garden completely immersed him in the elements of nature: a breath of air, a ray of sunshine, the chirping of a sparrow, a drop of dew, a raindrop, and a blade of grass expressed the glory of creation and they came together with his love, mingling with the nourishment of the earth. His mind was lost in the questions posed by Bashu and was forged in the growth of the rose, in the scent of its petals, in the withering that left the petals at the base of the stem. He joined with the mystery of life in its alternation with death to return to life again. His view was attached to *chaenomeles*, which glowed with life, even when it immersed in the sleep of winter. His heart beat with the cherry blossom that opened up to the rays of the sun and the April showers. His sense of smell was lost in the scent of violets in the grass. He was enchanted with the incessant gurgling of the water in the ditch.

The idyll diluted the desire of knowledge and gave rise to an ecstatic stupor of mind, awakened only to the alienating stresses of koans proposed by Bashu. His body, which became strong as a result of the physical exercise he did before and after meditation, was part of creation: earth, air, fire, water, wind, leaves, and grass. The harmony of creation was the glory of his God and struck a chord inside him that was at one with the wind.

One morning he went into the garden and found it completely destroyed: broken branches, uprooted trees, flower beds overturned. It seemed that a whirlwind had

demonstrate his/her understanding (Deshimaru, 1977b, p. 80).

struck, but only in his garden. An irresistible impulse led him to curse the Creation that raged against him. Due to his grief he slumped to the ground exhausted, almost dazed. He lay there for a long time, perhaps unconscious. A steady hand woke him, taking his arm and gently lifting him up. "You have much work to do. The mulberry is waiting for you and you need to mow the grass. Why did you stop? Maybe you don't like working in the garden?"

"No, Master." He wanted to continue to rail against the world, but was dismayed by the piercing glance of Bashu.

"Do you think the garden had become part of you?"

"Yes, Master, maybe you are right."

"You should care for the garden of heaven that neither tornadoes nor hurricanes can destroy. Plants, flowers, and fruits follow the cycle of life: they are born, they grow, they are eaten or torn, and die away. You cannot take possession of life. The plants are not yours, but they belong to all of us: air, water, earth, fire, wind ... and tornadoes. Your care for them is love, which is a gift, and also your care for yourself."

"Master, forgive me. I am guilty of attachment to worldly objects, presumption and omnipotence."

"Who are you asking to forgive you? Just ask yourself. I am not your Master, but you can meet him now: amid the damaged plants, the water flooding the land, and the pain in your heart. Here! Let the water invade you, too. In abandoning thought and in the confusion of the mind there is a state of grace."

"Thank you, Master," Okano said, looking for the calm and consoling eyes of Bashu, but he was already far away.

After a few months the garden was different from before and the signs of the hurricane were no more to be seen. It flourished and came back to life, oblivious and indifferent, as nature is blind, first a friend then an enemy, first creative, then destructive. With the transformation of the garden something had changed in Okano. He was into things, yet divorced from them. Here is the mystery of man, who was in and out of the world. However, he did not know the exact meaning of change. He did not perceive exactly where the turn of the path began and where the thread of his thoughts broke off.

In the evening he meditated for a long time and nothing happened. He did not expect anything. Perhaps what he hoped to discover had already come true or it would never have happened more. It was precluded to him because of his faith. Still, he expected the same, but what was to happen instead? He did not know any more, and yearning for knowledge did not fill him more. It was what he was: flesh, blood, heartbeat, the breath of his lungs, seagulls, waves, rock and sand. Without boundaries in contact with the outside world, it was a life forgetful of the past and alien from the future. This was the present flow of water, here and now, neither before nor after.

One night a beam of moonlight entered his room while he was meditating and almost dazzled him. A moth came in with the moonbeam and flew towards the candle, burning its wings. A sharp pain went through him and felt like the hole of a veil of ignorance. He got up and wrote the following verses.

The garden in flower
devastated by the hurricane
has left nothing.

The moon danced
many times in the room
never changing my thinking.

Darkness became
light through a moth
that flew in and burnt its wings.

The wings on fire
shook the stern reeds
veils of clarity.

There one deciphers
the law, which enshrines
jumps of digits.

The next day he went to Bashu. Even before Okano spoke, Bashu said, "The sickle is ready and the grain is ripe. It is time for the harvest."[15] Okano bent over in silence, in the throes of uncontrollable emotion that melted in the absolute calm of emptiness. He had nothing to add. There was no need for words because they had already said everything: from eye to eye, from heart to heart, and from body to body. He left in the hands of Bashu the page written during the night, as a gift, a memento, a witness. Then he walked slowly towards the entrance, towards the world, towards the exit, which was the entrance to the prayer never forgotten.

---

[15] "*The Perfect Way (Tao) is without difficulty/ save that it avoids picking up and choosing/ only when you stop liking and disliking/ will all be clearly understood/ .../ Do not worry about the right and wrong / .../ It is the sickness of the mind*" (Watts, 1957, p. 127). See also Mark (4.29).

39. The way of research

"Why is it that the more you look for something, the less you find it?"

"Because you do not look for it really."

"What, then, is the way to look for?"

"To look for not looking for."

40. To become a fair person

One day the young Nakata Sumiko presented himself to Bashu. "Master, let me be one of your disciples. I want to become a fair person."

"You have the wrong address. This is not a beauty centre," Bashu replied jokingly.

"Forgive me. Do you not want me with you, perhaps? I just want to be fair inside, of course."

"Have you taken a look at yourself? We do not know where to start. Go ahead," Bashu continued, on the same note. Sumiko's eyes widened. His eyes sparkled. He was determined to persevere in his intention. However, he had no choice, but to go away. He took his leave of Bashu with a deep bow, "Thank you, Master. Now I know the way I should take: To go back to go forward because the doors were closed to me."

Sumiko reflected for a long time. During the day he worked the fields with his father, concentrating on doing, and in the evening he studied the books of Zen, focusing on thinking. His reading was useful, but even more the manual labour was healthy. Digging the earth and breaking into a sweat was like entering into communion with the earth and the dust. Sowing rice was like fertilizing the earth and making it a generous friend. Watering the garden with buckets of water drawn from the well was like quenching the thirst of souls who longed for life. Weeding the soybean field was like removing the obstacles to the development of the good and useful against the bad and useless, yet so indispensable to the ups and downs of life: The usefulness of the useless. Through his work, the desire to learn Zen was strengthened in him. The air was always on the move, many forces gave it movement, from his breath to the wind. This aroused in him a sense of the ebb and flow, immobility and mobility. Immutability was an illusion or just a desire of the man who could not move in harmony with the evolution of nature. All this enabled him to reflect more deeply on the meaning of his life. He returned, therefore, to Bashu starting, "Master, I want to become a fair person. I beg you to allow me to be one of your disciples."

"Why? Are you by chance a mean person?"

"No," Sumiko said with firmness, "but you can always improve yourself."

"Or get worse. It is like going back to go forward," said Bashu, reframing the issue.

"Ah," Sumiko said, "I understand. I will go back to return where I am, here, at the right time" and in his heart he knew that he struggled uselessly in the void of words. He knew that only going down the valley would he meet calmer and slower waters. He returned to his daily chores in the family. He dug the land, he sowed rice and soybeans, he weeded the land in the spring, he harvested the crops in the summer, he drew water from the well to quench the thirst of the plants in the garden. In the sultry heat of summer, he went down to the valley of desire more and more, immersing himself in the things he did, vibrating strings that sounded for him always the same refrain: "To become a fair person". As a result, he went back again to Bashu, once again telling him, "Master! I want to become a fair person, who I am, who I was, who I will be. My path goes through here, but it will lead there. The Master can show it to me or not show it to me, because it is already laid out for me."

"You sing it and you play it. If you think so, you can sit where your pathway leads. Therefore, you should already know the place." Bashu bowed and walked away. Sumiko instinctively walked toward the place that was waiting for him. Just after coming in, he settled down and took a piece of paper on which he wrote the following verses.

The spade has turned the earth
the sickle has reaped the ears
the water has nourished the aspirations

but the sweat only has scraped away
the scales from the eyes and the efforts
have torn away the veil.

Now silence opens intricate paths
and trust inundates all my life.

I dig, so, without a spade, I reap
without a sickle, and chaos does not stop
the dance of longing for peace.[16]

---

[16] The poet and calligrapher Japanese Aizu Yaichi (1881-1956) once wrote to a friend: "*My dear friend acting and thinking calmly and with care at all times, keeping your heart at rest, I want to become a fair person*" (Aoyama, 1990, p. 99). The title and the story have something in common with the expression of Aizu Yaichi, because they use the same phrase, but also they contain different perspectives on the religious, metaphysical, and psychological level.

41. Sensations of sunset

"I like the sunset. It gives me a feeling of eternity, yet it only lasts a few minutes," a monk said to Bashu.

"Eternity lasts only a moment," Bashu said, "but nobody knows it."

"I know, though, that the sunset will return. Tomorrow or another day, it will come back with its watercolour tints that delight the eyes, with its endless fantasies of lights that illuminate the heart, with the feeling of the end that does not end, with the infinite that catches you in your finitude" the monk answered with conviction.

"Yes, but it will never be the same as the previous sunset," Bashu objected.

"Yes, but my feeling of eternity is always the same."

"You see, the sunset in the sky is more natural than the sunset of our feelings."

42. Colours of sunset

"The colours of the sunset are sweet and engaging," a novice said to Bashu. "They pierce the eyes, reaching to the heart. They remind you that the being is wonderful and the wonder is greater than the previous one just when the being is going to vanish. The melancholy of the sunset is a subtle and warm rain that permeates the skin to raise awareness of contact with the world. The farewell to the daily routine, already completed, is dissolved in the air that falls asleep. Master, why does everything go down?"

"Why does everything go up? You should ask."

"The dawn is different. The colours of dawn are sparkling in the air because they throb with nuances of the rainbow before the waking life, they are pressing in a kaleidoscopic environment because they ring long and loud triangles of dreams. They are drumming in our ears because they impress the rhythm of the heartbeat to the blood, they are overwhelming because they arrive as waves on the barriers of laziness," the novice continued.

"The colours of the sunset are no different from the colours of dawn. You look at them only from a different perspective," Bashu suggested.

"What is the best observation point to avoid the mental distortion of the colours, which enchant you, leaving you swept away in an ecstasy of unlimited space?"

"It is the point of view of colour."

43. Perseverance

"Is perseverance useless, if enlightenment is awarded at random?" a disciple, who practised the art of archery, asked Bashu. But Bashu did not answer and the disciple continued. "Why should we suffer the rigours of harsh discipline, when we are subject only to the whim of Fate?"

"Sometimes, even uselessness has its use," Bashu replied, with a vague indolence.

"In what sense, Master, can uselessness be of use?"

"If you had not trained in archery and had never attempted to hit the bull's eye with an arrow, maybe you wouldn't be able even to draw the bow. If you were able to draw the bow, presumably you would not have hit the target, let alone the bull's eye. You could have hit it by chance, but it would have been only by chance, not by design." There was a pause in the conversation. Then, the monk broke the silence and interjected a question with a dejected tone, "If chance governs events, then there is nothing certain in life."

"We limit chance through the exercise of discipline, without presumptions or expectations, but only perseverance gives us the strength to cross the empty and the full of one's own path."

"How can we cross the empty and full, when the empty does not exist, and the full does not have gates?" the disciple said.

"That is the point, to cross without crossing."

44. Circular Ethics

A young man, Yokohata Keishi, was staying in a Christian monastery because he was interested in ethics as a means to find the right way among many others. He aimed to pursue good and combat evil, but he could not find a satisfactory path. The paths of words led him up a steep slope and then back down again, disappearing out of sight, while he was seeking a point of convergence towards perfection, and equilibrium between aponia and ataraxia. He travelled through an impenetrable maze of knots that he was unable to untie. It was impossible to think of an ethic that was not just a convention. Absolute and universal concepts, with respect to the actual needs of life, reflected the gap between dream and reality, between being and ought-to-be. He repeated to himself continuously the terms of the questions, but he could not find a convincing synthesis.

The pleasures of the flesh were not good because the senses gave rise to an illusion and led the spirit away from the straight and narrow. Enjoyment, desire, and the pleasures of the flesh were not evil in themselves. In fact, they were an integral part of the order of nature that God had created, and what He had created necessarily had to be good. Nature and pleasure were a force for the good, but they were not the ultimate aim because sensuality was an illusion. Once satisfied, pleasures faded away and sensuality sought new kinds of satisfaction. The fulfilment of the senses was felt only when it occurred and immediately after the act, sensuality gave way to new needs. Sensuality was like a spring that had to be replenished at all times so as not to dry out. The pleasures of the flesh existed only in the present and needed to be restrained to achieve a peaceful and happy existence. At the same time, this insight struck him as childish as life seemed a continuous attempt to control, leaving him ensnared, imprisoned and mortified. Restraining the pleasures of the flesh was not the rule for everyone: Ascetics limited their pleasure for the greater good, but what was the point of considering this a good practice in a universal sense? Had the senses not been given to us to enjoy to the full? Was their aim not to capture the beauty of nature, to convey the energy of the world into the soul, and to reflect the greater glory of God?

Reason was often contrasted to the satisfaction of the senses, but reason was not a good thing either, because it was corrupt and impotent. He knew that. The virtues that were dianoetic, based on reflection and prudence, were debased because they were founded on reason that could never dominate the impulses and passions of the flesh. Believing it was possible to do so was a form of corruption, because it denoted the sin of pride. Only the grace of God and faith in Him could help to resist the temptations of the flesh. Otherwise, failure was inevitable. Would it be better to be passive, waiting to be surprised by grace? Of course not! Passivity was sloth. It was necessary to live by the virtues of faith, hope, and charity, prudence, fortitude, justice and temperance, in the knowledge that individuals were weak and fragile, subject to temptation. Reason alone – order, measure, and balance – could not bear the pain of life. The motto should be: Neither sink into hedonism nor to base action on reason. The intellectual capacity of the soul, manifested in contemplation, was supposed to lead to ecstasy and beatitude in the afterlife. The promise of salvation was held out to all, regardless of the degree of learning they had achieved.

Eternal happiness did not concern only reason, but also the body, and man in his totality. The resurrection of the flesh was a fact. Man was saved in his entirety, including the body and soul. The afterlife granted perfect knowledge, but also enjoyment of the senses. It was complete happiness, but without passion because the passions tormented the mind and the body, resulting in a life without recollections and without expectations. Could there be any enjoyment without passion? No, he said to himself, because the state of beatitude –

typical of the afterlife – was without thrills or exaltations, with no soul or body. The state of this world needed a fusion of passion and reason, intimate contact and sound reasoning. Was this the secret of happiness? Maybe, maybe not. He did not know.

Earthly happiness could not be an absolute good, and although everyone pursued it with anxiety and trepidation, it did not represent the goal to be pursued in life, because it led to perdition. People often sacrificed their own identity and the serenity of their heart on the altar of happiness. Neither hedonism nor reason alone produced happiness. He believed that only an alchemical combination of the two resulted in the reaction between opposites, lighting the fire that brought together reason and the senses. They were always worldly goods subject to the erosion of time, impermanence, illusion, and the betrayal of expectations because man was not autonomous and could never accomplish anything without the grace of God. Virtue was essential in itself and expressed man's ability to act, regenerated by grace and for the love of God, the ultimate goal to enter the gates of heaven and return to the Garden of Eden. If man was not autonomous, what was the use of free will? So many questions, so many inadequate answers.

These questions gave rise to a dichotomy between the pure soul, untouched by sin, and the stained soul, with nature corrupted by sin. The pure soul, associated with the Garden of Eden, combined reason and the senses in perfect harmony, but it was restricted to a primordial state of virtue and pleasure. The stained soul, associated with earthly pleasure, separated reason from the senses, but it knew intense pleasure and the agony of pain, with a contrast between being and ought-to-be. People suffered in this world, but what for? For the supreme good, ineffable and incorruptible, and for beatitude, intangible and invisible.

Only true faith could overcome the conflict between trust and distrust, doubt and certainty, questions and answers. The reward for the faithful was to hold on to their faith, but who could ensure everlasting joy in the afterlife? No one! Suppose the reward was only a mental construct with no basis in reality. What was the use of believing in a mortifying idea which required suffering as a necessary step for salvation? So much worry for nothing and so much sacrifice in vain! How was it possible to justify eternal punishment in hell for falling into temptation? Was there no imbalance between grief and guilt? An eternal punishment for making a mistake: What a cruel God! Heaven and hell were of this world, and the other world was an artifice, satisfying the pride of those aiming at being the best and most deserving! For Keishi, the worst enemy of the self was the self itself, both at an individual and a collective level. Man was an enemy to man, conscience was his executioner. "The truth shall set you free", it was said, but no-one could reveal the truth. Conscience was a torturer. Keishi was tired of this vicious circle. On a cold winter day, he left the Christian monastery and went to speak to Bashu, saying, "Master, I want to learn to understand good and evil. Teach me Zen, please!"

"Go back where you came from, to find out about good and evil," he answered and retired to his room. Keishi wanted to scream in response to such arrogance, but sat down and waited for him to come out again. He could not explain why he was there suffering in the cold, but he sat down and waited patiently for Bashu. When he eventually came out of the room, Keishi pleaded with him, "Master, I need to learn to understand the world. Allow me to become one of your disciples."

"You need to understand the world to be here, but you cannot gain the understanding you need. Go back where you came from." Keishi was overcome with anger, and he almost wanted to bite his tongue and cut it into pieces but he stood there and waited for Bashu, patiently suffering in the cold all night long. Bashu returned in the morning. Keishi, with a persuasive tone, approached him again, asking, "Teacher, I beg you humbly to allow me into the dojo. I need to meditate."

"Your pride is at odds with your words."

"There you are, Master, teach me humility and unity of words." Then Keishi fell silent, staring Bashu straight in the eye.

"You have learned all about hypocrisy, but words will not save you."

"Master, just the aporia of the propositions tore my mind apart."

Bashu was unable to conceal his annoyance and Keishi regretted speaking as he did. However, Bashu said, "If you want to stay, dig a hole over there." The mocking tone irritated Keishi and he asked resentfully, "What is the use of digging a hole, Master?"

"In order to have a hole," he said, disappearing behind the door.

Keishi worked hard and enthusiastically: pickaxe and shovel, shovel and pickaxe. The hole was waist deep and his brow was dripping with sweat. A voice startled him. "Now, fill it in." He turned slowly, but Bashu was already far away. He had just finished filling it in when Bashu said abruptly, "Did I not ask you to dig a hole? Come on! Dig." He wanted to throw the pickaxe and shovel aside and scream out of disappointment, but he continued to work with enthusiasm. He was still digging hard when the voice of Bashu boomed at him, "You have earned your lunch" and with a nod he called him into the kitchen. Keishi queued up with the others, he took his bowl, he filled it, he found a bench, and sat down apart from the others. When he looked at the bowl again, it was empty. He wanted to curse the disciple who had made a fool of him; but he could not say anything, and continued to meditate. He went to *dokusan* with equanimity. In the past, his heart would have been full of anger, and he would have been kicking everything, mad as a mule, due to the injustice and harassment. He came in and said simply. "The foreign body seeks a harmony that does not exist."

"The foreign body seeks it among strangers, perhaps? You say you know that it does not exist but now you can find it."

"Can we look for something that does not exist?"

"If you seek it, you can find it" Bashu insisted.

"What do I find, if it is nowhere to be seen?"

"What you bring to me, I will return to you."

"What do you give me back, if it does not exist?"

"What you take away when you leave us," Bashu concluded, dismissing him.

Keishi came away feeling confused. He meditated day and night, but all the tasks he performed were pointless. He dug ditches, and sometimes filled them in. He cleaned his room and, shortly after, immediately someone dirtied it and he had to clean it up again. He filled the bowl and someone emptied it. Every now and then someone threw ash or buckets of water over their head. Of course, he felt like a foreign body. Every time, he felt a surge of anger in his stomach, but it did not come to the surface, that was a blanket of soporific fog interspersed with stars. One day he went to *dokusan* saying, "Master, stubbornness spurred me to resistance, but how can I ask you about good and evil? Why should I ask you considering you are stranger to my beliefs? Only you can help me to look for something authentic, real, surrounded by the ignorance of everything."

"You are on the way towards perfect truth," Bashu answered.

"How can I walk in the truth, if I am a prisoner of thought? How can I be on the way towards perfect truth, if I am unable to tell the difference between good and evil? How can I make my choices if I no longer know what is right and wrong?"

"Telling the difference between good and evil is a presumption of the mind."

"Do we not need to think, then, to know?"

"I never said that you should not think, but that you can think without thinking."

"What does that mean? That thought cannot comprehend existence, and that one cannot exist without thinking? That good and evil cannot be told apart? That human behaviour cannot be improved?"

"If only good existed, how would you know that that was good? Without comparing it with evil, what kind of good is that?"

"The existence of good is not the matter for discussion, but the pursuit of good, because only action aimed at good can improve the world and cleanse the soul."

"If no-one was dedicated to evil, we would lose the notion of what evil is. If the night did not follow the day, we would have a different world: bright and dull."

"So illusion is the belief in the inexorable march towards progress? Vanity is the hope of pursuing good? Is the exercise of virtue only of utilitarian value?"

"If you exercise virtue only for the reward that you hope to gain, as your belief indicates, then it is only of utilitarianism value and it would be an act of presumption. I say to you, 'Go further, even if you are not from here.' I say to you again, 'Hold on to remain empty-handed, earn to be poor, learn to discover your own ignorance.' After all, drinking allows you to live and then to be thirsty again."

Keishi bowed his head, thanked him, and went out in silence. He knew that Bashu was disinclined to talk and he was grateful for the words which Bashu uttered. He was happy. He was greatly surprised when someone told him his bowl would be empty at lunchtime, in the evening someone told the same thing again and over the following days. He went to *dokusan* intending to complain, but when he reached the threshold he only said, "Master, I am hungry, but I can also die of satiety."

"Then eat to stay hungry."

"I want to free myself of the need to eat."

"The need not to eat is just as strong."

"My mind eats into my body and my body engulfs my mind, where will my salvation be?"

"Not here, but in your faith," Bashu said, pointing to the door. "Your longing brought you to me in order to bring you back to yourself. It led you to cross borders to send you back home, because the foreign land does not suit you. You will find salvation when you lose it. Be poor to be rich, because the rich man has already received his reward. Blessed are the last, as they shall be the first." (Matthew 19.30, 20.16, Mark 10.31, Luke 6.24, 13.30)

"I knew the truth, but experiencing it is something different. I have nothing of my own, except the consciousness of my reflexes, bringing a vision together with all the others, for a reflection that is both necessary and unnecessary."

"You run away from yourself in order to find yourself."

"Everything goes round in circles: Good and evil chase after each other to complete the mosaic of reality. Free choice is the hub of non-choice and vice versa." Bashu interrupted him, "So many words, too many words for both of us. Go back to work." Then Bashu sent him away with a strength which struck him to the core of his being.

Keishi returned to his usual occupation in a different mood. He did not know why, but he did not reflect on the causes of the change. Thinking undermined thinking, reason eroded reasoning, reality eluded perception, feeling faded with the sensations.

He carried out many unnecessary tasks, but they reinvigorated him instead of diminishing his dignity. The rhythm of the seasons went with the rhythm of his digging and vice versa. The garden was always in a state of ferment: the plants were blooming, the bees were buzzing around, and the sparrows reared broods in the hedge. One day the chicks emerged from the nest and made their first attempts to fly, hopping from branch to branch, tweeting, crying for help, chirping with joy. Suddenly a hawk swooped down on them and grabbed the hen bird causing terror and making the others dart back into the hedgerow in silence. It seemed like an eternity, but only a few minutes went by, when the music of life began again: flying, pirouettes, jumping, twittering amid the murmur of the bees and the other sounds in the hedgerow. Keishi was astonished at the cruelty of nature, at the tragic relationship between pain and joy. The truth appeared before his eyes without a veil, without reasoning, without contradictions. It appeared along the road he had to take. The moment of departure had come. He went to Bashu to take his leave,

"Sparrows in flight
a hawk drops the veil
*   on the song in sky.*

> *Good and evil*
> *like the left hand and the right*
> *   one side is the other.*

Around in circles
always along the two verses:
*   It is a carousel in the world.*

I follow the path
standing still in the cosmos
*   where the path is."*

Keishi bowed and thanked him, "Master, my questions have been answered, albeit without answers. As a result my questions have been solved or appear unimportant. Good and evil pursue each other and I go with them as if in a spiral. To be part of them without ultimate goals is the purpose of pursuing the good, while knowing evil. Too many words for a final farewell, but I hope you will make an exception for outsiders." Keishi went on his way and saw a once solemn face now giving him an ecstatic look.

"You came as a stranger who did not know, while he believed he knew. Now you are leaving no more as a stranger, believing you do not know even what you really know."

45. Joy and pain

One day a man presented himself to Bashu, saying, "Are there universal laws, that apply to all men?"

"Do you need to know the answer?"

"I can tell the difference between good and evil. Joy comes from that which is good, pain comes from evil."

"What is universally good, is good for everyone. What is universally evil, is evil for everyone."

"If you do not know the universal truth, you cannot improve yourself and the world. Do we need to seek perfection? Do we need to attain enlightenment? Telling the difference between good and evil should be the starting point."

"And is death good or evil?" The boy hesitated. "Come on, answer! If it is good, you are dead. If it is evil, you are dead too."

"How can I know, if I do not establish the nature of good and evil, or I do not understand joy and pain?" The boy replied filled with consternation. Bashu struck the boy hard on the shoulder with his *keisaku*, adding, "Now you know what pain is." Reeling from the blow, the boy retorted. "Now that I know where it is, how can I walk away from it?"

"By going forward to meet it."

"After meeting it, how can I get rid of it?"

"By going beyond it."

"Is there not a risk that I will meet it again immediately or later on?" Bashu struck him hard, with his *keisaku*, on the other shoulder, "Now you have met it again, but the last one is already past." The boy, confused and bristling with indignation, said to him, "Now both my shoulders are hurting."

"That's right! You cannot tell the difference between the two. Your mind is in a state of confusion."

"How can I learn to tell the difference between various situations?"

"By not distinguishing between them, but welcoming them."

"Even when you hit me?"

"Yes! In a while you will feel a great relief, almost pleasure, and a sweet lightness in your body."

"Then, should I go back for some more?" the young man asked with impertinence.

"Yes, if you liked it."

46. Outward and return journey

One day a mature couple presented themselves to Bashu and said, "Here we are."

"Here you are," Bashu replied. A leaden silence followed. Suddenly, the couple broke the silence by asking, "Do you have nothing to tell us?"

"The words are yours."

"Let us go!" The man said to the woman, starting to shake, while she mumbled something that was barely audible. "The judge told us to come here. We were hoping you would help us." Her husband had tried to silence her, saying continually, "Shut up! Shut up!"

"What is the matter?"

"Our daughter-in-law lives alone with her two children," and the woman's face lit up. "She makes them suffer so much," she added with a grimace, a mixture of disapproval and disgust. "They are so dear to us but she is not a good mother. She does not take care of them and they are dirty and neglected. They never wash nor comb their hair. They do not attend school and are always out of the house, often alone. She cannot bring up them. She is not able to be their mother. In our view, it would be right to give them to us. Since we lost our son, our house has been so empty: no son, no daughter-in-law, no grandchildren. Our son is not dead, he ran away with another woman and we have no idea where he is. Since then, life has been a living hell. Our daughter-in-law went to live alone, but she neglects the children."

"Why did you come here?" Bashu said, interrupting her.

"The judge asked us to come."

"Advised you to or told you to?"

"Both." The husband looked at her with hatred.

"And you expect me to help you get your grandchildren back?"

"Yes, I do."

"You are mistaken." The woman tried to react, out of pride. "Oh! Master, why do you treat us like this? Tell me, why does that wicked woman make her children suffer so much?"

"Does she really make the children suffer?"

"Yes, she does! She is never with them."

"And why is she not with them?"

"Because she is not a good mother. She thinks only of her work."

"Does she think only of her work because she loves her job or because she loves her children?"

"Because she does not want to be with her children," she said, beaming.

"Ah yes? And what would her children have to eat if she did not have a job?" The woman flushed, but her eyes remained proud and determined, "That is her problem! She brought them in the world, not us! Children need love and we can give it to them, so we want them to live with us."

"Do the grandchildren agree?" The woman said ruefully. "We did not ask them, but they will do as they are told."

"They need their parents, not their grandparents. You do not love your grandchildren because you know nothing about them. You want them with you, for your own sake. If you loved them, you would help their mother to enable her to stay home with them. Get out of here, you petrified souls." The man, who had watched with growing excitement, dashed towards Bashu, who struck him with his stick. The man was surprised. He did not expect such a reaction from one known as Master! He picked himself up almost immediately intending to go for him again but Bashu was nowhere to be seen.

The couple came back, but the woman was upset. Over the next few days, she could not sleep but cried and cried. The husband cursed his daughter-in-law and tried to placate his wife, but great was her grief and nothing could fill the emptiness in her life. In the middle of the night, the woman stood up, went back to Bashu, and waited for him at his door.

She wanted to attack him to knock some sense into him, and to bring him round to her point of view, but when he came out, she just whimpered, "Please help me."

"Ah yes?"

"Why is your heart so cruel? I asked you for help and you refuse to help me"

"Your grandchildren are fine where they are."

"Do you really think so? Now I need help not to get my grandchildren back, but to get myself back."

"Ah yes?"

"Yes," she replied with determination mixed with despair. She saw the scepticism on Bashu's face yet she found the strength to rebel against him. "Why are you so impassive? Do you think I am incapable of finding myself? Am I too old?"

"You are projecting your impassivity onto me. Everyone has the ability to help themselves. You can understand yourself at any age."

"Then why do you not reach out to me? Why do not you help me?" she said sadly.

"I can help you only if you help yourself."

"What kind of master are you, then? Are you here just to think your enigmatic thoughts, to impress everybody with your wisdom, to be reassured of your superiority? Do you think you can change the world through words?"

"Your pride has got the better of you. It is time for you to leave."

"No! I will not move." Bashu moved forward as if to strike her with the stick and she burst into tears. When she recovered, he was nowhere to be seen. The woman stood there in tears. Time flowed around her head and her heart. Suddenly Bashu appeared and she rushed to him, "Master, I beg you. Help me! Teach me to know myself. Let me stay here with you."

"We need a cook. If you want, you can work in the kitchen." Her disappointment was evident. She did not know whether to go away or stay. She had always had a domestic.

The kitchen was a complete mystery to her, but she agreed to serve the community. Shortly after, her husband came to beg her to return home, but she resisted fiercely and ignored his threats. She took part in all the work and over time felt a certain relief. She did not know why this happened. Perhaps, closed in there, she could get away from the world, from illusions, from appearances, from the desires that were unrelated to the self. Perhaps the isolation helped her to concentrate on herself, slowly forgetting her strong feelings, and all forms of desire. Perhaps the meditation at the *dojo* penetrated her inner mind and body.

One day, without knowing how or why, she became convinced it was time to leave. No enlightenment, no nirvana, no cathartic event, no revelation. Leaving the community was the result of the harmony between feeling and action derived from meditation, the union between reason and emotion, her inner silence reflecting the external silence. The woman went to her last *dokusan*. "Nothing special has happened but I can see clearly now. Time has moved on the heat of the kitchen. Where is my enlightenment? If you do not look for it, you will not find it. Maybe it is an illusion of the mind. Perhaps it is the desire to satisfy the senses, to gain power over things."

"Your words show you have crossed the frontier. You did not want to cross that frontier."

"I have gone into the beyond, but I have come back. Now I can go home. Whether here or there I will always find the centre of the self."

"And you are ready now to face the journey there and back!"

47. Savouring peace

"What is the meaning of the verse: '*To save life it must be destroyed*'?[17] Maybe we need to throw it away in order to keep it?" a young man asked Bashu.

"If you forget it in a drawer, it is like throwing it away."

"I do not forget it because I always have it with me."

"But if you do not throw it away, you cannot look for it."

"Why should I look for something that I already have?"

"He who does not look does not find."

"I find it all the time because I love it too much to do without it," the young man proclaimed satisfied.

"You love it to the point of not living with it"

"No! I always try to savour the best of life, to get the most out of it," the young man replied.

"You think you know how to savour it, but you do not think about how to do so."

"If I throw it away, what do I savour?"

"Peace."

---

[17] "*To save life it must be destroyed. When utterly destroyed, one dwells for the first time in peace.*" Verse of the Zenrin (Watts, 1957, p. 165). See also Masini (1988, p. 31, n. 73), John (12.24-25) and Mathew (16.25). This text came to light subsequent to the writing of the dialogue.

48. Having confidence

"How can we have confidence in the world, where suddenly a cataclysm can come and upset our life? How can we have faith in the future, when a disease can come along and change our life? How can we have hope, when man can carry out despicable actions towards the world and himself, undermining our certainties? How can we live without confidence?" a man asked Bashu.

"By focusing less on confidence, you can attain confidence."

"Master, they are just words! The facts are different and the words do not explain reality. If you read them literally, then you see only a part of it. If you interpret them, then you see only the reflection of your mind. What should I do, Master?"

"The stone of the road."[18]

---

[18] Bashu's response can be compared with that of Joshu in Mumon (1957, p. 63, no. 38). Just in the spirit of dialogue, the two answers are different and are the same inside and outside the ambit discussed. In "*The Oak Tree in the Front Garden*" by Joshu, the "*Stone of the road*" is mentioned for its symbolic and semantic implications. The significance of words is to be seen also in the comment of Mumon (1957, pp. 51, 63, no. 27 and no. 38).

49. The suffering of God

"God is eternal and compared to Him, life is just an instant, nothing. The suffering of God who became man is an instant, nothing! What is the significance of all this?" a young Christian monk asked Bashu.

"Look at the sky," Bashu replied, turning his gaze towards the heavens.

"Are you telling me it does not concern you?"

"You said it."

"Do you think it a trivial question or are you avoiding the answer? You are missing an opportunity, in any case," the monk said defiantly.

"Wonder, then, why He made Himself man," Bashu replied almost with a tone of mockery.

"I do not care for received wisdom. I just want to know what the value is of Him becoming man, suffering as a man, if suffering is a nothing for Him."

"Even for you, suffering is nothing, if you go beyond received wisdom."

50. Consciousness

"I exist in consciousness, consciousness exists in me. If I am contained by something, I cannot understand it, because I am smaller than it is. If the container is inside what it contains, how can the contents contain the container? If consciousness is both the contents and the container, how can I experience it, Master?" a young man asked Bashu. At that point Bashu responded by striking the young man's shoulder and then asked him, "Tell me about the consciousness that you are experiencing: Is it the container or the contents?"

"This is not the experience I am looking for. I was wondering how to test it in an abstract sense."

"Before asking how to experience it, maybe you should ask yourself where your conscience is."

"It is in the mind, but when I seek consciousness, there is nothing but the mind, and when I seek the mind, there is nothing but consciousness. How may I get out of this vicious circle?"

"Clear your mind and you will find consciousness, clear your consciousness and you will find the mind. Get rid of both and you will find yourself."

"How can I get rid of them? If they are in me, I must also get rid of myself."

"That would not be such a bad thing," Bashu quipped, but the young man continued to speak with trepidation. "How can I get rid of them, if they are unlimited, while I am limited?"

"Where is your limit?" Bashu pressed.

"It is in everything, Master, in action and thought, mostly. I perceive my existence only with the mind, I see myself only through consciousness. How can I exist without them?"

"By being rather than existing, you will discover existence."

51. The dream of the eagle

"Master, I dreamt I was riding an eagle and climbing the steep slope of a gully. What does it mean?" a disciple asked Bashu.

"You are not here to dream, but to work. Go on with you."

The disciple went back to work, but the next day he was still there, "Master, I still dreamt of riding an eagle with a pure heart that shed light. What does it mean?"

"You are not here to dream, but to realize. Go on with you."

The disciple went back to work, but the next day he was there again, "Master, I still dreamt of riding an eagle with a pure heart that could look at the light. Then, suddenly, the light turned me into a stone that emanated heat. What does it mean?"

"Go tell somebody else."

"I tell you only what I dream of."

"Do you dream what you wish for, or do you wish for what you dream of?"

"The two questions seem to me the same thing. Wishes and dreams merge together. I aspire to spiritual life, and dream of the road that leads me towards my goal. If the dream repeats itself, does it mean that I carry on along the straight road to the achievement of the good?" the disciple asked him.

"The dream is the obverse and reverse. Ask yourself when the truth is hidden in its opposite. The eagle is cruel and rapacious, domineering over the other birds in flight. It is a symbol of pride and oppression. And it personifies initiation, because it goes from one world to another. Where do you place yourself?"

"If I do not know the two worlds that the eagle flies between, how can I locate myself?"

"Go back to work and learn about the world you encounter in your dreams."

The disciple dug the earth with intense dedication, and drenched in sweat he turned these questions over in his mind: "What is the world I encounter?", "How?", "Why?" He did not see the world and as a result he could not find answers. The eagle came at night, and attracted his attention. Sometimes he looked up with joy; at other times he feared being unseated and falling down. Every night he concentrated on his dreams, convincing himself that he would not have dreamed about an eagle, but a tiger, a butterfly, a flower, a spring, a stone. No! What do you expect? The eagle appeared again in his dream and, after swooping down, gripped him in its powerful claws, and flew up towards the sky. He found himself riding the eagle and turned into something like a star. After the first few nights, he began to react, struggling and screaming out loud. Finally, he woke up all sweaty in bed.

One day he was going down a country lane where a shepherd was grazing his flock. Suddenly an eagle appeared in the sky, which caught sight of a lamb among the flock and, swooping down, gripped it in its powerful claws. The shepherd ran towards the eagle, but he got there too late. The eagle dragged away the lamb, that was already dead, as it made not a whimper.

That night he did not try to drive away the usual dream, as he was so upset by what he had seen during the day. He slept like a lamb, ready to meet his own bird of prey. Like the other time, the eagle came and snatched him away but this time he did not react, and he felt a surge of strength from somewhere inside, releasing the energy he needed to express himself. "Who are you? Which world do you come from? Why?" The eagle did not speak, but the answers came across to him, as if it were speaking. "Who are you?" "I am the ferryman, from east to west and back again, I am the thunder and the lightning, the earth and the sky, fire and water."

Then he asked, "Where are you from?" Then came the answers. "I come from another universe. I come from the realm of the shadow, bearing a mirror to see what is right, this way and that."

Again another question, "Why are you here?", and another answer, "I am looking for you, but you do not find me. You find me and you do not meet me. You are avoiding me so as not to speak to me." The answers were not words spoken, but feelings transmitted to his heart and mind, doors opening over the abyss in the light and dark. He was not alert but half-asleep. It was not in contrast, but in agreement. The flight continued up to an indefinite height. Suddenly it stopped in a void, while he nestled among the feathers. He did not turn into stone. He did not feel a hot flush. Only emptiness wafted through the space containing his being. He felt like he was in a rainbow of blurred fog. Colours and sounds permeated his skin as he awoke in a state of exhaustion.

The next night he did not expect anything. He lay down without thinking and slept soundly: For the first time the eagle did not appear. Also the following nights the eagle did not appear in his dreams, and he felt free. He was in one world or the other or he was neither in one nor the other. His dreams faded in his sleep. Now he had to learn how to cope with the daily journey on the path to truth and freedom.

One day he went to see Bashu, who immediately understood his mood, "The eagle flew over the border, now everything is free in your thoughts." The disciple opened up his heart to this message. He greeted Bashu by bowing his head and summing up his experience,

> "*I encountered silence*
> *and emerged from confusion*
> *I talked and understood the centre.*"

52. The goal of the street

"Where does the way lead us?" the young student, Suzume, asked another student at the school of Bashu.

"The way does not lead us. We are the ones who lead the way." Somewhat puzzled, Suzume said. "Where do we lead it, then?"

"We lead it within us," the other replied with deference. Annoyed, Suzume insisted. "How can we lead the way within us, if we are not the way?" The other smiled and retorted. "You cannot lead the way where there is already a way. Only where there is a no way, can you lead the way." Suzume quietly submitted to the remark of the other student and went away in a state of desolation, almost irritated at being put down. Then, Suzume went to Bashu for clarification. "Master, what is the way?"

"The unspeakable in the breath of a syllable."

"If it is unspeakable, there is no syllable to name it. So why do we talk about it?" he replied in a resentful tone.

"It was you that talked about it."

"Master, I do not know if I can manage it. I discussed this with a student and I was unable to find the words to answer him. I felt I was cornered," Suzume said dejectedly.

"Ah! I see. You intend to compete! But if you do not find the words, put them to one side." The student went away dissatisfied, but he was determined to take up the matter with the other student. One day he met his antagonist and asked him, "How can we be the way and not the way?"

"The rains falls then evaporates back into the sky. The caterpillar turns into a chrysalis then into a butterfly. The woodpecker is keen to catch larvae. Children run in the garden. By walking you are the way, but by stopping you are not the way. That is why you are the way and not the way. Beware, if you are walking you are still, but if you keep still, you are walking."

"If I keep walking, then what is the way?"

"The way is like the flight of the heron."

He was taken aback, but he was reluctant to show he had not understood. The other student aggravated the situation with another remark. "If you have not yet understood, ask the heron." Almost downcast, he felt faint. After a brief silence, he pulled himself together and laughed.

"Why are you laughing?" the other student asked Suzume.

"Because I asked the heron."

"And what did it tell you?"

"It cannot be repeated through the words of man."

"Tell me with other words, then."

"Craic, ca. Craic, ca."[19]

---

[19] To the ordinary cry of heron is a penetrating "craic", while the cry of alarm is a short "ca" (Brehm, 1983, p. 351). Note that the two verses, contradicting each other, show two opposite aspects of life. In this case they are not said at random, but reveal the jump taken by Suzume in the understanding of the dualism of the intellect that divides reality to represent and use it in practice (Suzuki, 1950, p. 48).

53. The being who is not

One day Semi, a young student of Bashu, presented himself to the master, and complained to him, "Here I have only dug the garden and not learned anything." Bashu tried to drown out his voice with an "Ah," but the disciple went on without stopping, concentrating on what he was saying, "Thought is ever-changing, flowing, elusive. Only being has a basis in itself and can affect thought." Bashu banged his *keisaku* hard on a stone and asked, "What is this?"

"A stone," Semi said.

"A stone, so it is."

"A being that is not a being, because a stone does not think," he replied, pleased that he had found a retort.

"To think the stone is no more than to think of the stone," Bashu answered dismissively.

"Master, why are you not kind to me? Why do you not explain anything?" Bashu hit him hard with his *keisaku* and with a smile escorted him out of the door, exclaiming, "Do not say that you have not learned anything."

Semi reflected on the situation all night long, sulking about the outcome of the conversation and glad to have had the attention of the teacher. He said that if the stone existed, the stone lived. If the stone lived, it could think, but nobody had ever known this before and as a result it was useless. What distinguished the stone from a plant or a cat? Nothing. Even a plant lived in the air, like a stone, whereas a cat darted around with its heart beating fast like a human. Who was able to say that a plant did not dream about a ray of sunlight or a cat did not dream about a trip into space? Who was able to say that the plant did not reflect on its immobility? That the cat did not pity its feline existence or was glad about it? The explanation was easy on the human conscience, which distinguished mankind from other beings. Even the conscience, however, was a concept conceived by the human mind for self-congratulation. What evidence did humans have to deny the consciousness of the plant or the cat? None, but man persisted in believing that other beings did not have consciousness, persevering in this presumption. Everyone lived, therefore, Zen.

Regardless of others, humans moved through space and time and come into communion with the divine. Living Zen was to become Buddha through meditation, releasing the self-consciousness and the awareness of being. Did the mind become an obstacle through the taxonomy of reality? It was necessary to abandon the reason of nothing to reason upon the whole. He seemed to grasp the truth that he did not catch, but the two verbs did not express his feelings. To grasp and to catch denoted predatory actions or voracity, both wholly unsuitable. The tension grew. The mind became confused. He fell unconscious. He came to his senses with a new vision and everything was as before. He walked to the garden. On the way he met Bashu. It seemed that he was waiting for him; but Semi went on ahead, almost without greeting him. After overtaking him, Bashu turned and landed a blow on Semi's other shoulder. He turned calmly and said, "There is a reason for this blow. There is no reason for me to leave without saying goodbye."

"Where is the narrow path that you are walking down?" Bashu said.

"Yesterday you beat me on the shoulder to make me learn," Semi answered.

"Now what is your response?"

"Now I have a pain in the other shoulder."

Bashu spoke to him gently,

"The sun rose red from Fujiama
the water runs down to the sea which calls it
the broody hen gathers her chicks."

Semi replied to him in the same tone,

*"The man hangs his mat out of the window
the rain gathers on the streets
and the chick follows the path of inspiration."*

With a deep bow he took leave of Bashu, who smiled at him from the depth of his heart.

54. Faith

Bashu was invited to stay at the monastery of Katsumura Okano. One day there came a novice who asked Okano, "Don Katsumura, why do you say that faith will change your life? I believe in God but nothing has changed: I get up in the morning, I work the land, eat, sleep, and have the same apprehensions that I had in the past. I pray, but I get the impression of repeating words that make no difference to my feelings: Words that feed only hope for a distant future."

"Your words are full of sound and fury signifying nothing. If you pray from the heart, you will be aware of a real difference," Okano said.

"To believe is to follow the Word. To believe is to recognize that there is one God and then there is the Trinity. To believe is to know that salvation is within our reach. To believe is to have faith."

"You believe, but you have no faith," Okano replied.

"I believe, that means I have faith. Otherwise, what is faith?"

"Faith is an experience that transcends consciousness and the intellect. It is not enough to accept the Word and to carry it in your heart, but you must bring it to life that turns an existence without reason into a reason to exist, and your breath at every moment will be the miracle. Only then can you live with the absolute and the void in a simultaneous encounter."

"I do not understand, Don. If faith was an experience, then we should ask ourselves what kind of experience. Different men would have different experiences, while faith itself is the same for everyone and the object of faith is the same. Otherwise, faith is nothing because it is anything, in other words it is all different experiences, though all similar. If faith is not a belief in the Word of God, then what is it?"

"The wind that blows through the wall," Bashu replied.

"How can the wind blow through the wall?" the novice asked, bewildered.

"Ask the wall," Bashu answered, waving him away with his hand.

55. Afterlife justice

"Father," a parishioner began, to draw the attention of Okano, who was sitting nearby Bashu. With a nod, Okano invited the man to speak. "There is a thought in my mind that haunts me. On reflection, being a Christian is tiring. You have to forgive those who harm you, to be merciful to others, to love your neighbour even when he or she is wicked, to be ready to donate a roll of cloth to those who ask you for your cloak, to turn and offer your left cheek to someone who slaps you on the right cheek (Mathew 5.39). You have to commit yourself completely because the reward, that is, salvation in the afterlife, is worth all the required sacrifice. But be careful! Even those who do not make any sacrifices, but repent of their sins, will be forgiven and will have exactly the same reward. What is the use, then, of making the effort? Would it not be better to take the easy way, acting according to convenience?"

"Yes, you have to act according to your true wishes. To efface your true self is a sin," Okano answered.

"I cannot believe it, because it is the opposite of what is written and preached. If that which I desire is improper, immoral, harmful to others, can I desire it without sin?"

"If you do not know that what you are doing is improper, immoral or harmful, it is not a sin. If you are aware of it, why do you want to do it anyway?"

"Because it makes me feel better. You feel almost like a doormat as a Christian. The point is, I do not want to be considered stupid. I do not want to give up something for nothing."

"Living a Christian life should lead to tranquillity and joy. If it does not, what kind of Christian are you?" Bashu asked, interrupting him.

"The others call themselves Christians, but act on the basis of personal motives, that have no justification in

Christianity. They hope to have their reward in the end, all the same," the man replied resentfully.

"Be guided by your heart, not by the behaviour of others."

"I cannot ignore the fact that I live in this world," the man continued. "To make sacrifices without any reward makes no sense. Those who make mistakes should be made to pay the price. They should perish in hell suffering terrible pain and gnashing their teeth."

"You do not understand the meaning of love. You are arrogant, haughty, and selfish," Bashu remarked, beating his *keisaku* on the man's foot, to the astonishment of Okano. "Go and meditate on those who are hypocrites who look at the speck of dust in their brother's eye, without seeing the plank in their own eye." (Matthew 7.3-5) Suffering from the blow and greatly offended, he wanted to respond to Bashu, but was overwhelmed by his authority. However, he could not stifle the urge to reply. "I am just thirsty for justice! It is written that those who do not bear witness to the bridegroom with wedding clothes, will be cast out of the banquet (A wedding-feast: Matthew 22.1-14, Luke 14.15-24); those who does not go to meet the bridegroom with lighted lamps will be disregarded and will never know neither the day nor the hour (Ten girls and their lamps: Matthew 25.1-13)."

"Obstinate men will suffer as a result of their obstinacy. The judgement we pass on others will be passed also on ourselves," Bashu said, interrupting him.

"I have no fear for myself," the man shot back.

"We will all receive the wages we deserve as the worker is worthy of his hire." (Workers in the vineyard: Matthew 20.1-16), Okano remarked with a conciliatory tone. Bashu added, "Your pay will be equal to the mercy of your heart, to the charity that you have shown, and your love for neighbour."

"Do you think you are better than me? You will not even be in heaven, and your wisdom will be your enemy in that judgment," the man responded promptly.

"It will be no more of an enemy than your dullness," Bashu retorted, waving him away with his hand.

56. The salvation of all

"Father," a novice said to Okano, "If the goodness of God is infinite, then He should forgive our misdeeds and our mistakes. He is infinitely merciful and should forgive all our sins. Why should a place of perdition, like hell, exist for the eternal punishment of those who have sinned? Is that right?"

"Do not forget that he is also infinitely fair," Okano remarked.

"Yes, but his infinite love cannot allow even one of his children to be lost forever. Love conquers all," the novice said triumphantly.

"Love does not always bring forth love. Some reject it. A free individual cannot be coerced either by infinite responsibility, or by immense solicitude, or by the spirit of understanding," Okano objected.

"Individuals may be free, but who would choose eternal damnation? If you knew for certain that you were destined for hell, you would change your ways. I do not think anybody could be so stubborn. People make mistakes out of ignorance."

"We hope God will save them all," Okano said and the novice's face lit up. Bashu had been listening to the conversation and he asked the monk, "Where is your salvation?" Bewildered by the question, he answered. "In heaven."

"Then why do you care so much about what happens on earth?"

"Because only here can you work towards salvation in heaven."

"Even salvation on earth has to be earned."

"There is no salvation on earth. We are just passing through. Life on earth is the transition towards salvation in heaven," the friar said, on an apologetic note.

"If you do not save yourself on the earth, you cannot save yourself in heaven."

"But how can I save myself on earth?"

"Ask the sky," Bashu concluded.

The novice went on. "I was not interested in how people can save themselves, but rather in the criteria by which some are saved and others are damned. Will we all be saved?"

"Yes," and then added "Here!" with a nod as if to send him away. The novice, tenacious and curious, went on. "If we will all be saved, in any case, I do not need to follow the right way. But if we will be saved here, then we need to consider how to save ourselves. In your opinion, how can I be saved?"

This would have appeared to be rather bold, had it not been for his sincerity and keen interest. Bashu asked him to come closer and, with something verging on complicity, said, "Following the right way enables you to feel here and now the joy of the afterlife."

The novice replied. "How can the metamorphosis of the caterpillar and the chrysalis take place before his death? Show me the other way, if it exists, and I will follow it."

"You will following the way and rise again after death." Then he moved a little closer to him. Suddenly Bashu grabbed him by the ear and squeezed it. He leaned in close to bring the ear to his mouth, then whispered, "There is no indication in words. The Word is clear by itself. Find it by yourself."

57. Syncretism

"I heard your talk," Asago, a preacher of the monastery of Okano, said to Bashu. "It seems to me that you are a syncretist."

"What do you mean?"

"You want to bring together the heaven and the earth, but they are totally separate. You want to join the land and the sea, but they are totally different. You want to heat all three elements with fire, but they are fireproof."

"Heaven contains the earth and water and fire. The earth contains water and fire. Fire dies in the water. It is not me that joins them, but nature."

"Perhaps you mean that we ourselves need to see the contradictions? That is to say that we do not know how to understand the totality of the world? I am wondering how it is possible to be a Buddhist and a Christian at the same time," Asago said.

"That is not what I said. I am a Buddhist only. Maybe you say one thing to mean another."

"No, I am speaking only about you."

"Do you want I turn this into a contest?"

"Why not?"

"Well, I never said what you say: sometimes I am a Buddhist, sometimes I am a Christian, sometimes I am both."

"There is only one truth and all other versions are false," Asago retorted.

"Your holistic view is a thing of beauty, but I wonder how you can see different versions of the truth."

"Different versions of the truth cannot exist. There is only one way, as there is only one life. You hear much talk of joining disparate elements together but it just leads to contamination, corruption, emptiness. I am in favour of distinguishing: I distinguish, therefore, I identify the truth. To borrow a phrase from Descartes: I distinguish, therefore, I am," Asago concluded.

"And this distinction is necessary for you or for the truth?"

"It is necessary not only for me, but for the truth. We follow the right way and we need to spread the Word because we want to save humanity."

"That is only partially right. Communion also comes from that which divides us, perhaps irreparably, because that which divides is important, as much as what unites. How can you talk if the other person has preconceived beliefs and will not listen to anybody else? Then it is not a dialogue, but a monologue that is disrespectful of others," Bashu said, interrupting him.

"The distinction is required by any institution that does not allow for deviations. It is essential to know the official truth. Think of what would happen if we thought that the truth was everywhere. Everyone would build their own system, or drift from one belief to another, or observe only the parts of different religions that suited them," Asago went on.

"Institutional truth is no longer the truth of the heart," Bashu added.

"Maybe, but only institutions endure over time. We would still have paganism or sectarianism, if institutions had not been created."

"Anyone who criticizes institutional truth, then, is a heretic? Anyone who seeks innovative ideas, should be tried for heresy and burnt at the stake even today? An institution cannot tolerate gaps or openings because it risks its existence as well as its credibility. Where is the courage of the daily practice of the Word among the people? Those who are thirsty are ready to drink from the fountain of the truth," Bashu said, making a point.

"Our aim is to be both among the people and among the institutions. We want society to adopt rules based on the spirit of our beliefs."

"Would it not be better for social rules to be less influenced by your ideas? If the law makes religion compulsory, what is the point of complying with the law? If you do not recognize the spiritual value of a certain type of behaviour, are you not indirectly practising violence and also guilty of hypocrisy?"

Asago opened his eyes wide and appeared to be puzzled. What could he say in response to all this? The ground was crumbling beneath his feet. He mumbled something saying he felt deeply that his efforts had to be directed to change society. He could not abandon it to secularism, but he understood the need for the freedom of choice of the individual and respect for diversity. Then he thought he had found the right response. "Can I ignore a man who is heading towards the precipice? I have a duty to stop him."

"The precipice we speak of is not visible to the senses. A man's existence is an act of faith. If someone does not have faith, you cannot give it to him. Is faith not an act of grace? A gift?" Bashu concluded. According to the Word of God we must wake up because the time is approaching, indeed, it is already here (John 4.23).

A long silence followed. Asago stood there without batting an eyelid. He needed comfort, relief, a breath of fresh air. Bashu spread his arms with a sweeping gesture, smiled, bowed, and said, "We have raised a lot of dust," and stamped his feet on the ground as if shaking the dust off, then walked away (Matthew 10.12-14).

"Peace be with you," Asago said, bowing humbly.

Like a faint echo, almost indistinct, the answer came. "And with your Spirit."

58. Men and cicadas

"Master," the disciple Zakuro said to Bashu, "sometimes I feel a sense of melancholy that puts me in touch with nature. The sound of the rain falling goes to my head, the birdsong enchants me with its melody. Then, I think of the evil that afflicts us and I despair, especially for the evil caused by man. I cannot stand to see men so blind, so foolish. Do you listen to cicadas when they sing? When someone is distressed, he racks his brain, he kicks and stamps his foot, then shouts himself hoarse, just like a cicada," he said, pointing to a dead cicada on the ground.

"It once sang cheerfully."

"Yes it sang all day! But what was the point? Listen to them singing and think how ephemeral their life is." As he was speaking Bashu struck him on his left shoulder with a stick. "Aaah! You hurt me," he shouted, turning and looking at his shoulder. When he looked up, Bashu had moved on. The pain did not distract him from the sense of nothingness that permeated human action. All worries vanish as the body and mind decay. Yet, human behaviour was not always consistent with the highest principles of ethics. There was no gate to go through the wall of the blindness. Meditation was only a weak defence against the rising tide against the breakwater, but how can we find the strength to face the storm of life? What can we do when nature rushes at us? What can we do when someone attacks us with brute force, deception and wickedness? Nothing. We can only seek to mitigate the blows, to extinguish the resentment and the wickedness. While he was tormented by these thoughts, he looked round gazed into the void. Bashu kept an eye on him and as he was concerned about his state of mind the next day he went to him and asked him, "How are you?"

"Fine," he replied, "except for the pain in my shoulder."

"Then, have the other worries and evils vanished?"

"No, they have not! Not at all: the water moves forward and the rocks tumble into the waves." Zakuro did not manage to finish what he was saying, because Bashu struck him on his right shoulder then walked away. Over the next two days, Zakuro stayed in his room to meditate. He was filled with despair and loneliness, far away from everyone and everything. His life seemed to flow along a river-bed different from its own. From then on he had to find a way to break free. He was with the sky that connected with the earth. There was a way that led further on and he had to follow it. The rule was to enjoy each day without being confined by it, and to welcome the light while remaining in the dark. Everything was thoughts and words, no experience, no inner strength. On the third day he came out and found Bashu in front of him, as if he had been waiting for him.

"How are you?" Bashu asked him.

"I cannot tell the right shoulder from the left: The pain is the same on both sides."

"Where are your worries today?"

"My shoulders were hurting, but not anymore. The cicadas sang mercilessly all night long, so I did not sleep. Now I am hungry and I need some breakfast."

"Where are your sandals? You are barefoot," Bashu said.

"Look! The sun has been up for a long time, and but you can still see a sliver of the moon."

"There is a good smell of coffee. Sit down at the table and break your fast."

59. The mechanic and the accident

A young motor mechanic realized as he came into the garage that he could no longer work there. It was the first day after his convalescence and a sense of nausea gripped his stomach. Yet, in the beginning he had been keen to work in the garage. He had qualified as a mechanic and had immediately found work at the garage, where he repaired and tuned high-performance cars. He remembered enjoying his work with a sense of humility, that was a source of wonder to himself and others. He was happy to do any task, even the most routine jobs, but to tune up an engine was what he liked most. His heart missed a beat at every roar of the engine. Everything he did seemed a miracle and he was always happy to do a repair for his friends. On Saturday evening, they went out to enjoy themselves. They drove fast, as an antidote to their boredom, and their sense of anonymity.

He felt tired and uneasy, but was reluctant to show it. He was with friends, but he needed to keep his feelings of weakness to himself. If you worked hard all week, how could you stay awake until five in the morning at the weekend and still hold a conversation and keep up with what was going on? It did not take much. Just a little help! He felt alone, but could not even pay attention to these feelings, because there was a force inside him that was like a volcano about to erupt. After work he had to get it off his chest. He was tempted by new experience, close encounters, and unknown sensations. With all the pent-up energy in his body, he could not understand why his friends wanted to drive at break-neck speed through the streets. But that was what they did, and he followed suit. Driving at top speed, the trees on the roadside flashed by in a second and his heart beat in sync with the engine. Driving more slowly seemed like standing still or acting as cowards, but the risks and the adrenaline were too high. The price to be paid for all this was too high. It happened to some of his friends whose lives had come abruptly to an end.

It was too late to go back, too late to think about what had not been and should have or could have been. The crash had shown him his dark impulses and he was painfully aware of the scar on his face, the broken bones, and the young lives that had been thrown away. Fate had struck: His friends had seemed immortal but had been flattened like bugs on the windscreen. "I will find something else to do: I can train as a baker, plumber, or electrician. I will do something else, but I can't stay here. I can't stay here anymore," he said to himself. He had to pick up the pieces and put himself back together. On the one hand, he longed to find peace. On the other, the instinct to live was stronger. He was tempted to go down the same road. How could he persist on the road to perdition?

He felt he had been born in the wrong century.

Years ago he could have dedicated his energies to politics. Today he might be able to do voluntary work to help other people. He had the strength to do it, but he lacked the capacity: When he came across a person who was suffering he was unable to cope with the grief and understood that there were no words to comfort him. Perhaps the words were there, but he could not find them. Now he understood this all the more, because no one could console him for his disfigurement. Desolation and apathy took hold of him and were starting to devastate his body and mind.

One day he heard that there was a *sesshin*[20] open to all, at the monastery of Bashu.

---

[20] Sesshin, literally meaning "touching the heart-mind", is a period of one or more days of collective life dedicated to zazen in a Zen Monastery. During a sesshin those taking part devote themselves almost exclusively to zazen. The term is also translated as "spiritual concentration" or improperly as "gathering the mind". Most of the time is dedicated to meditation and those taking part remain in perfect silence, away from the world, for the entire duration.

He went there with no hope. In that condition he was ready to try anything, even though he knew it was useless. He was ready to listen to fortune tellers, chiromancers, pranotherapists, magicians, sorcerers, priests and charlatans. He followed the teachings carefully to avoid mistakes, but his heart was as hard as a rock. He listened in silence to the sermon: Nothing happened to him. The days went by and another meeting was arranged. Like an automaton he told them that he wanted to take part in the next *sesshin*. The days went by without him finding a job, and he continued to be overcome by anguish. Then something began to stir inside him. At last the days of the *sesshin* came and he discovered a kind of peace that he had never known. At the end of the session he asked Bashu for a meeting. He explained the problem and expressed an intention to stay with him for a while, not to learn the Zen, but to live a little with Zen.

"Yes," answered Bashu "you can stay on condition you make yourself useful."

"Thank you, Master. I am ready to do anything."

"This is what you need to do. There is a workshop near here that could do with your help: The young mechanics there could learn a lot from you."

"Master, you are asking me to do exactly what I cannot do."

"You see only one side of the issue," and struck his right hand with a stick. "Your hands are the engine of your mind. How can your mind work if your hands remain idle?"

"Master, you do not understand. It pains me to go into the workshop."

"Your eyes are dull, at one time they were bright. If you do not want to work, so be it. You are free to choose, but I want that you to go there," then struck him a blow on the other hand, and walked away. The young man was left alone to ponder on what to do. Should he go away or stay there? If he stayed there, should he go to the workshop or remain idle? What could he do? He remained motionless for a long time and gathered all his energies and thoughts. He hoped that the solution would become clear, but after many hours nothing came to mind. Going away meant running away from his responsibility, so he had no alternative. He had to stay, but he did not want to go to the workshop. That meant he had to make himself useful some other way. He needed time to figure out what to do and spent a long time in meditation, idleness and pain.

One day a disciple came and asked him, at the request of Bashu, to come over to the kitchen to repair some broken equipment. This was like a breath of fresh air for him. He went over and after a while he had dealt with the fault, but he had the impression that the equipment had been tampered with. After that, he was called on repeatedly to repair, to replace, and to adjust doors, kitchen equipment and farm implements. The disciples did not make friends with him, but they were kind to him and this gave him a sense of well-being. All of a sudden he was not called on anymore. He returned to his state of calm and everything was going smoothly but he got the impression that somebody else was doing the repairs. With no duties to attend to, he was able to devote himself entirely to himself but he was also overcome by a sense of loneliness and uselessness. He spent hours looking around at the sky, the birds, crops, and insects. The ants fascinated him: tireless workers, fighters, highly disciplined. One day he stepped on an ants' nest and stood watching the carnage: One of the ants, though wounded, was trying to drag a grain of wheat into the nest. This struck him, leaving him totally absorbed and gazing into the void for a long time. He realized that Bashu was near him and he tried to make an excuse, "Master, I am sorry. I am a burden on the community."

"Your burden is less than that of the grain of wheat dragged by the ant. Giving and taking are two sides of the same coin. If there is no-one to receive a gift, then nobody could give."

"Master, I am undeserving. I see the scar on my face as a warning. I have to make a move that does not come from my consciousness, or from my weary body."

"Where are your feet?" Bashu asked him and the young man was left confused by the change of the subject and by the question.

"I do not understand," he replied, but without realizing what was happening, he felt himself grabbed by the hair and felt his head being pressed down towards his feet. He would never have thought that this man, minute as he was, would have such an iron grip. His hair seemed to tear away from the scalp and he could not utter a word because of the pain. He just murmured, "They are here, in front of my eyes."

"Let your head be there too," then he pushed him forward and walked away, leaving the young man in a state of confusion with two phrases in his mind: head and feet together, feet and head together. It was a kind of obsession. He heard a noise like an engine, a car engine that sang and joined his head and feet: That engine was himself, it was like the movement of a car, joining together his head and his feet, vision and movement, thought and action. It was as if a ray of light piercing the darkness, a gentle gust of wind, a breath of fresh air. Now he breathed in deeply and the fog lifted, as his feelings became clearer. As he breathed in deeply, his thoughts became clearer and the arguments more convincing. The next day he went to Bashu, who greeted him with a warm smile, saying, "Does the wounded ant want to bring his grain of wheat?"

"Master, the barn is full. Is there still room in the workshop for the last grain? Time has not gone by in vain and in a year I will take my leave."

"Do not plan ahead. Fruit ripens in its own time. You will know when it is time to go, and then you will go." The young man wanted to express his worries about his work, his anxieties, his memories, his lack of confidence, but he bowed his head, smiled, and thanked him. The next day he went to work. When he got to the doorway he froze. His workmates, all together, were waiting for him, but his eyes grew dim and his limbs were heavy and unresponsive. It seemed that the others were motionless, waiting patiently for him to make his move. But he was all alone and no longer had the strength to move forward.

Suddenly, he felt a sharp blow on his right shoulder-blade, which almost made him fall over. Soon after, another sharp blow landed on his left shoulder-blade, rebalancing him and pushing him forward. He found himself going through the doorway. He heard Bashu's voice behind him. "Your feet and your head together. Take courage. *Kwatz!*" Bashu shouted so loud as to make the onlookers turn round in surprise.

"Now he is yours. Go to work."

This was a place where he could find the energy to be himself. The disciples welcomed him and accompanied him in a quiet corner, where they sat for meditation. Then they began to work in silence, without encouraging him, as if he did not exist. That evening, at the end of working day, they sat together to meditate all night. The next day, they stopped work in the evening and went to the *dojo*. A similar pattern was repeated on the third day, but for him it was less of a burden. After a while, they began to involve him by giving him tasks to do, which he accomplished with no difficulty, to his surprise. The work went on for a few months. Day after day, the will to work and to be useful returned to him. The traumatic events of the past were behind him even though they were not forgotten. He was alive. The past was instructive, not destructive. It was a warning, not a millstone round his neck. Finally, he went to Bashu, to thank him, "Master, the grain has germinated. The wheat is grown and is ready to cut. The harvest is waiting. The wounded ant has recovered.

The wounded face
changed my outlook
and my desires.

I saw wrong
a stroke of sword pushed
over the block.

I went back slowly
to my daily routine
the usual view.

I owe so much to you
and in the verse that I drink
I pay and receive."

"The words I gave you were like water that has now come back as wine for your heart to drink. I am satisfied," said Bashu, bidding him farewell.

60. The defeat

Sugo, a young man, introduced himself to Bashu and explained that he was suffering but he had no idea why. He felt uneasy and wanted to give vent to his frustrations. "I need someone to guide me, to give me a hand. Please help me."

"I can only help you if you help yourself. If you have been unable to help yourself till now, how can I help you?"

"I have tried to help myself, by plucking up the courage to come to you," Sugo replied emphatically and added, "You always win."

"If this is a challenge, then I have already lost."

"Are you really afraid of losing or is this a case of false modesty?" Sugo asked.

"You do not know what you are talking about," Bashu replied, but Sugo would not listen to him, going on with his monologue. Finally, he concluded, "No! It is false modesty to taste sweet victory."

"Is it possible to talk to someone who is unwilling to listen? For there to be a winner, there must be at least one loser. Without someone being defeated, who can be the winner?" Bashu asked, almost menacingly.

"Do not tell me your tall stories. The answer is: Nobody! But this is not the case, because every time one of your disciples attains enlightenment, it is the glory of the Master. Every time you help somebody, you are the winner. For every winner there is a loser! There is a loser, and it is Evil. The winner is Good over Evil."

"You are overestimating my powers. When a disciple attains enlightenment, he looks into himself and gains awareness of his inner self. Then he can live each moment as if it were the last. Who can enable him to acquire that kind of insight? He can only do it himself. That means the merit is his alone. What are the benefits for the Master? None! It is an experience that goes beyond experience and there is no merit in the realization of a *satori*. Whenever my help has any effect, it is a success for the person being helped because I cannot do anything for him unless he so desires."

"You sidestep embarrassing questions, but you cannot tell me such stories." Then he looked downcast and, frightened and trembling, he burst out. "Master, help me! I am afraid! I feel paralyzed and unable to move my legs. I feel a heavy weight bearing down on my chest. I feel the shadow of death on my back." Sugo's face was beaded with sweat, his legs were shaking, and he collapsed. Bashu picked him up and took him to an inner room, entrusting him to the disciples. A few days later, Sugo returned to Bashu and apologized, asking for help again.

"Are you ready to help yourself?" Bashu asked.

"Yes," replied Sugo "But I am afraid of failing, of being too weak. I am afraid of disappointing you."

"It is not my victory that matters, but yours. But do not think it is easy! There will be many defeats before you can win. We learn more from failure than from success. Every time you get lost, this helps you to find yourself later."

"Then I will help you to understand what defeat feels like and how to avoid it," said Sugo, looking despondent, not really replying to what Bashu had said.

"If you aspire to be a martyr, then that is your personal choice. But if you do not fight, if you do not make a commitment, you will learn nothing. You need to do the right thing."

"Thank you, Master, for your encouragement. But the emptiness in my stomach begins to exhaust me and I feel weak. What should I do?"

"If you are sick, go to the doctor. If you want to change, you can stay." Sugo did not reply, but bowed, took his leave, and withdrew. He intended to commit himself to the full, but his lack of strength let him down. He became increasingly distrustful, and his mood darkened. Meditation brought some relief, but he saw darkness all around him. Bashu watched and offered him some guidance and encouragement but Sugo continued to be blind and indifferent. Everything appeared to be gloomy. One day he observed a moving scene. A lark was flying from the nest, but suddenly it changed course and was captured by a hawk. The lark was carried away but the nest was safe. On hearing this story, Bashu told Sugo not to focus on appearances. "The lark sacrificed itself to save its brood. Our instinct to live is stronger than our inclination to die. Yet sometimes it falters. We must start from here to prevent gloom from hanging over us."

"Thank you, Master," Sugo said, mindful of the fragility of life.

One morning, the disciples were alarmed as Sugo had disappeared from his room. They brought the news to Bashu and looked for him everywhere. Darkness fell, and they were pained by his absence. The next day Bashu went with one of his disciples to view a cliff some way from the monastery. After a long search they found Sugo lifeless at the bottom of the precipice. He might have fallen down accidentally, while trying to negotiate the narrow path, or he might have thrown himself off the cliff on purpose.

"Today we have lost a brother and a battle," the disciple said.

"A hawk is flying high in the sky. If it swoops down to get food, it will rise again; if it swoops down because it failed to find any food, it will not rise again."

"The heart that lives in the shadows rots in the darkness. How could this be avoided, Master?" the disciple asked.

"When we see our goal, we can decide on the best course of action. But first we need to see our goal."

The disciple went on, "When we cannot get the desired results, then every word and action comes under scrutiny. All of this seems to have been written in the stars from the beginning, but maybe we should have worked harder to encourage him. We were unable to help him and we have to ask ourselves, where were we when he was here? Were we supportive and concerned about his well-being? Today I feel like him: His malaise has become mine. Today, Master, we need to be comforted for the loss of Sugo but even that will not be enough."

"He needed a new way of seeing. But how can you change the point of view of one who does not listen? Listening and seeing are one and the same thing."

"If he had listened to us, he would have been on the right path and would have just needed encouragement. He needed to open his heart to us. That was our goal, but we did not know how to achieve it. Master, forgive me. Are we really so powerless?"

"Perhaps we did not see him or we were simply unable to overcome the gulf that divided us. We need to strive to increase our knowledge. We need to find the strength to stand pain of this kind."

"Today we were defeated, Master."

"No, it was not our defeat, it was his! His defeat strikes deep inside us and we grieve for him."

61. Religion and society

A young Christian went to visit Okano, who was staying with Bashu at the monastery. During their conversation, he asked, "Father, our task is to spread the word among men, and our ideas should be embraced by society. If we could provide inspiration for our institutions, would not our actions be more deserving?"

"Maybe, but our purpose is to listen to hearts, not to dictate the rhythm at which they should beat. We should teach people how to find faith. We should speak to their conscience and promote the free experience of law rather than forced observance. We should testify, not dictate," answered Okano.

"Father, teaching the Way is not an alternative to taking action. We live in society and we ourselves are society. We should be free to profess our faith, our morals, our ethics, and our understanding of the Way. We think of the good of all people. We want everyone to attain it and act according to the principle of the common good."

"But we should not isolate those who do not embrace those principles."

"No, but if we acknowledge that Sunday is the day of rest, then everyone would be able to attend services and even those who do not believe in religion might take an interest in our beliefs. If social norms reflect religious principles, then everyone is led to follow the path of goodness, which is the way of salvation. It is for their sake."

"Rules of this kind can guide us, but they cannot force us. The more social norms break free from religious belief, the greater the value of faith as a free choice."

"A society permeated by faith is a more just society," the disciple argued.

"The law is the law, without forgiveness and without mercy. But can we sanction those who do not adopt religious principles?" Okano asked.

"Why not? The principles reflected in the law of God should be universally acceptable. I do not think anyone can be against the Ten Commandments."

"The man who does not honour his father or his mother commits a violation of God's law. Perhaps he will have a guilty conscience. But is this to be considered a criminal offence?" Okano replied.

"But the absence of religion increases greed, exploitation, and ingratitude. Compassion and respect fall by the wayside. The absence of religion leads to permissiveness. It makes us forget our duties to the older members of the family. It results in the use of drugs. It leads to divorce and abortion, deviating from the straight and narrow. We need to address all these things."

"The answer is to live life according to the Word. Render unto Caesar that which is Caesar's, render unto God that which is God's. There is a need for rules that apply to all of us and to persevere in the discipline of love."

Okano turned round and went on, "Father, I still have many questions about the social aims of religion, to improve men, to create a society permeated with love and kindness."

"So many questions, so many answers," said Bashu, who was seated nearby.

"Give me an example of such an answer, then," the young man replied defiantly, turning to Bashu.

"Your habit is too long and heavy," said Bashu enigmatically.

"Would you mean that I am crude and have ambitions that go beyond my abilities?" The disciple responded with an acrimonious tone. "We need answers to these questions in order to move forward and reach the desired goal, not vague comments and witty remarks."

Bashu responded with verve. "Your faith will fade away, when you have no more doubt, because faith is nourished by doubt. Where there is faith, there is a desire for knowledge. To doubt is to believe and to believe is to doubt. In fact, Christians have often caused others to behave in an opportunistic way out of ignorance or cowardice. They have encouraged people of other faiths to feign conversion, and have persecuted free thinkers. Devout persons have lost themselves in the object of their devotion and found faith where there was none. You are interested only in finding new disciples and not in their care. Unfortunately, proselytism generates division, not union. Therefore, we should not make recommendations on how to vote, for thirty pieces of silver."

"Aaah!" the young Christian interrupted him. "These are the usual claims and the usual accusations."

"However, you learn nothing from them, as you reject them", said Bashu, but the disciple went on. "I have so many genuine questions. Who should I turn to in order to deal with my doubts?"

"Ask that dog," he said, pointing to a dog that was wondering around the garden.

"Well, I asked the dog and he told me you are a dog. What do you have to say now?" the young man replied.

"Bow wow! Bow wow!" Bashu said with a voice higher than that of *kwatz*.

62. The happiness of stone

A man came up to Bashu in the street and asked him, "What is happiness?"

Bashu looked him deep in the eyes and replied with a broad smile, "What is happiness?"

"A question needs an answer, not a response repeating the question," he said with a tone of irritation.

"I have given you an answer."

"Answering the question by repeating the question is not an answer. Give me another one," he insisted with ill-concealed impatience.

"Happiness is blowing in the wind," Bashu said with his hands open. The man stood in Bashu's way and smiled ironically, asking again, "Please, tell me something more."

"The wind blows when you want it to but also when you do not. It changes direction and blows your sail the other way. Nothing is more changeable and impalpable than the wind. Nothing is more weak and relentless than that," Bashu retorted, trying to be patient.

"You do not want to answer, or rather, you do not know the answer and hide your ignorance behind words" he concluded, disheartened and angry. Then the man stamped his foot on the ground, as if to shake off the dust, and walked away in a huff.

The next day the man came up to Bashu again and asked him the same question, "What is happiness?"

"Happiness is stone," he replied, as he made his way down the street.

"You want to impress people with your understanding but you hide the emptiness of your mind. It cannot be stone and stone does not know happiness," he continued.

"Did the stone tell you?"

"Stone is inanimate and cannot be happy and neither has it the right to be it. You are indifferent, without love and respect for your fellow-men. Shame on you," he replied impatiently, taking his leave and turning in the opposite direction.

On the third day the man came up to Bashu again with the same question, "What is happiness?"

"Look over there," Bashu answered, turning his eyes to a wall dappled in sunlight.

"I am looking at you, not at the wall," he shot back.

"Look! I tell you. Happiness is lying in the sun, like that black cat on the wall."

"I am not a cat and I cannot lie in the sun like a cat. I asked you what happiness is. You are wise and you should know," the man said, with some irritation.

"Wisdom is not happiness and does not lead to the happiness you are seeking," Bashu said gently.

"I ask for what I want," continued the man, exasperated.

"It is not enough to ask for something, we need to seek it, but tell me why you are so troubled. You need to keep your pain on a short leash," Bashu replied affectionately, opening his arms to embrace him. Then the man blew into Bashu's face with all his strength and stormed off, stamping on the ground.

The next day the man was at Bashu's feet, following him like a shadow. Bashu ignored him and continued on his way. When he returned to the monastery, the man stood near the entrance clearly intending to stay there, lying in wait for the rest of the day and night. The next day he was there again, taciturn and melancholy. Bashu continued to ignore him. The third day he was still there, in front of the monastery, ready to follow him. Bashu took no notice of him. At the appropriate time, the man came forward and addressed him, "Why do you ignore the world around you?"

"If it is around me, then it is in me and therefore I do not ignore it," Bashu said calmly. The man bowed his head and went on. "I would like to learn about happiness."

"What have you learned from unhappiness?"

"Why do you always answer my question with a question?" he said irritated and exhausted.

"Do I always reply with a question?" Bashu asked.

"Your responses are like words in the wind. I have no way to understand them. Teach me how to understand," he pleaded.

"Stones know nothing about the language and yet they know happiness," Bashu replied defiantly.

"Let me come into the monastery to learn the happiness of stones and find a way of dealing with my pain."

"You may come into the monastery. You know when you come in but you do not know when you will leave because healing follows happiness. At the same time, happiness follows healing."

63. Improper promptness

A disciple, who had gone on an errand with Okano, came back to Bashu all breathless, saying, "Master, a misfortune has befallen us! It was Okano's fault. We were taking a large sum of money to the monastery near here, and as we made our way through the forest, two robbers assailed us and made us hand over the bag. I made as if to hand it over, but then I reacted, waging a fierce struggle with one of the robbers while the other managed to take possession of the bag. I tried to fight against both of them, while Okano stood aside and the robber who got hold of the bag managed to get away. I chased him, but he managed to get on his horse and gallop away. I was on foot and so I could not chase him anymore. If Okano had helped me, we would have taken good care of the money and carried out the task assigned us. But what did Okano do? He rushed to help the robber I had knocked to the ground. He revived him. He hugged him and apologized, while I chased his accomplice a short way. Then the robber I had knocked to the ground managed to get on his feet. He shoved Okano to the ground and fled. Okano is totally unreliable. He has many strange beliefs: forgiveness, turning the other cheek, the resurrection of the body, life after death. This is why he got us into trouble. He was so sorry for what happened that he stopped in the woods to pray and walked back alone. I wonder why Okano was asked to go with me. Could you not choose someone else?"

Bashu was silent and carried on walking. The disciple followed him in a state of agitation and insisted.

"Master, do you not say anything? We need to turn him out of the monastery because he leads us away from the right path."

"If someone leads you away from the right path, then you have already deviated from your principles. If you are not what you want to be, then you deviate from yourself only," Bashu replied affectionately.

"He made a detour towards the wood. I made a detour towards the monastery. Who was it that turned away from the right path?" he retorted proudly.

"The route through the forest is in the shadows. Where is the route that is dappled in sunlight?"

"Okano has his own beliefs to live by but this makes us vulnerable. The rabbit in the hole is not safe from the snake, nor is the rabbit in the woods safe from the falcon. We have a debt towards our brothers and we do not have the means to pay it off," the disciple said sternly.

In the meantime they had reached the *dojo* and Bashu opened the door with a solemn look on his face. The robber who had been helped by Okano was in the middle of the room, praying alongside the bag stolen in the woods.

"What debt are you talking about? Are you referring to the contents of that bag?" Bashu asked.

The disciple bowed his head and said contritely, "I beg forgiveness. I have sinned due to an excess of zeal. Love generates love. Who can say what that is worth?"

"Do not turn away from your path to take the different path shown to you by Okano."

64. Duality and unity

One day Bashu met Okano. He shook his hand firmly and asked. "If the right hand does not know what the left is doing, where is the unity of man?" Okano grimaced in pain, clenching his teeth and closing his eyes. When he opened them again, to his astonishment Bashu had disappeared. Bashu's question puzzled him and reminded him of a verse from the Bible, *"But when you do some act of charity, do not let your left hand know what your right hand is doing"* (Matthew 6.3). How could the right hand not know what the left hand was doing? It was impossible because the action was in the mind. It was well known that the verse from the Bible was a metaphor to teach that the good done to others should remain a secret, in other words, it should not be ostentatious.

He had to go beyond conventional thinking and contemplate the idea of the right hand not knowing what the left hand was doing and vice versa. Did such ignorance imply the absence of unity of man? If the answer was affirmative, then man no longer existed. If the answer was negative, then he would need to ascertain where the unity was located. In the mind? He felt that the path was becoming tortuous, but out of respect for Bashu he wanted to keep hush and show that he had understood the connection with his faith. At their first meeting Okano said. "Ostentation is like the peacock's tail because you see it even when it is not there, while discretion is like the breeze from the sea because you do not see it even when it is there." Bashu immediately responded, "The peahen passes unnoticed. The unity of man is neither in your word nor in your thinking," and walked away, but added. "If the right hand knows what the left hand is doing, is that ostentation?"

He turned, raising his right hand, "Look up there. In heaven there is a fluffy white cloud. My right hand knows because it saw it, but my left hand does not know it is there."

Okano continued to ponder on this, but he felt a tension, an unbearable pressure. There was a gap in his line of reasoning, perhaps due to the illusion of the union of opposites to transcend the dichotomy of things. Later, Bashu asked him, "What does the right hand know of the left hand?"

"The right hand does not need to know what the left hand is doing," Okano answered as if he had felt an electric shock. He put his right hand behind his back and held out his left hand with the palm turned up. Bashu struck a blow with his *keisaku* on the palm of the outstretched hand, then remarked. "Now only the left hand knows," and moved on, leaving him speechless.

He brought together his right hand and his left hand, and the distance between them was no greater than the thickness of a human hair. The right hand and the left hand ignored each other in the emptiness of the union and they recognized themselves in the fullness of division. Knowledge was lost in the myriad of insufficient explanations to understand the multiplicity of the world.

He spent the rest of the day and night turning this over in his mind. The next day, Bashu appeared before him and addressed him. "What does the left hand know of the right hand?" Okano bowed his head out of respect and was silent, but Bashu pressed him. "Are you telling me you have lost your tongue? Has the cat got it?"

"Yesterday my left hand hurt but now it does not hurt anymore. But I still do not know the answer to the riddle of the left hand and the right hand," Okano replied after a pause.

"The answer is to be found in the cat. Where are you?" Bashu asked with mockery.

"I am in my sandals dirty with the cloud of dust, blown in by the wind."

"The wind blows high in the clouds that sail before your eyes."

"The clouds are the sails, heading towards the harbour, where the swallows swoop down as if in a dream."

"The harbour is calling them. Dawn is upon us," and Bashu, dismissing Okano with a light touch of his *keisaku* on the left shoulder.

65. The departure

A disciple of Bashu approached Okano, who was gazing at the horizon. The disciple put his arm around Okano, and said to him. "How deep is the sky?" Okano replied while remaining immersed in his thoughts, "How high is your heart?"

"Is your heart not of this world?" the disciple asked, taking his arm away.

"My heart goes beyond the world, because it is in the world." Then he turned and said, "Do you need to tell me something about the world? Tell me now, without wasting time." Again the disciple put his arm round Okano and embraced him gently. "Okano, your father is dead."

A slight tremor ran through his body and tears began to roll down his face. The disciple took his arm away and said by way of consolation. "I am sorry, but you can be consoled because those who have departed this life, according to your belief, are reunited with the Father. This means it is a time of sadness but also of joy."

"Yes, it is true," replied Okano, fighting back the tears. "Those who have departed this life find God, whereas those who stay behind find no-one."

Okano carried on speaking with tears in his eyes. "Those who come go, and those who go come. Even our tears come and go."

"Why do you speak of crying?" The disciple did not manage to finish what he was saying, because Bashu slipped in between them. Bearing down on them, he said, "Why do you speak of crying?"

The disciple answered in a guttural voice from the position in which Bashu was holding him. "We talked about it before, because a good man has left us. We talk about it now, because my neck is hurting."

"Relief will follow the pain. Song will follow on from the tears. Look at the cherry tree covered in blossom in the orchard. It fills the entire field with light. Soon it will be heavy with fruit. In the end, the tree will shed its leaves in a semblance of death. It is past, present, and future. It comes and goes. It goes and comes." Then Bashu led them slowly into the orchard. Okano went in the opposite direction to the other disciple, mumbling in a low voice "My head aches, and a drowsy numbness pains my senses."

66. Looking for sense

"On examining a clock we see that it is different from any other, though just like any other clock from the same factory. To understand the true meaning of things we need to know whether there is a reality which is able to show their quiddity[21] and to redeem their appearance. The manifold becomes one," the disciple said, reflecting on the clock on the table before him, as he came in to have a *mondo* on the search for the meaning of things and life.

"Appearance is, and is not. Quiddity is an abstraction and it is empty. It does not exist. Do you exist?" Bashu asked.

"I see myself. Therefore, I exist," the student answered.

"The air is invisible, but it exists."

"The air exists, but I asked about something else," the disciple replied.

"I answered something else. You can go," and dismissed him, calling in another.

The next disciple came in, greeted him, and said, "The meaning of things lies in their Suchness[22] as the essence of a thing emerges from its individuality which allows it to be just what it is, and not something else. It makes no sense to look for a common sense of the whole, because you only need to

---

[21] The Latin term is "quidditas": a corresponding term in English might be "essence". The term is used in medieval philosophy to indicate the essence or form of a thing, in other words, what makes a thing what it is and not something else.

[22] "Suchness" is one way of indicating the Latin "*haecceitas*", where "*haec*" implies "*res*" and, therefore, "this thing". In English it may be termed "thisness". The other way is "haecceitus" which comes directly from the pronunciation of "*haecceitas*". The term was coined by John Duns Scotus (1266-1308), the philosopher of Suchness, and indicates the perfection of each being, referring to the specific nature of the individual, making him unique.

be in tune with your being. This means going from the subject to the object and vice versa. Relations with others and with the world around them are the meaning of things and life. This is something that is intrinsic to the thing itself."

"Is this quiddity?" Bashu interrupted him. The disciple was puzzled for a moment, then he continued. "Here I am. I examine the clock, a clock like many others, and yet in this moment, it is distinct from all others. Time and space are fused in my eyes. Together, time and space are the dimensions in which we are immersed. Space is the time in which we live. Time in this clock is expressed in this moment." Bashu interrupted him. "You all look at the clock, but you do not see the non-clock." Then he asked. "If everything is in this moment, then where can the non-clock be?" Bashu murmured, with an incomprehensible "*Tathata*"[23] and fell silent. The disciple waited for an answer. After a while, he asked. "Why do not you speak?"

"There is too much noise from all the words in this room," Bashu said.

"I asked for an answer, not a comment on the sounds in the room."

"I tell you that I have given it you. Now it is time for you to take your leave."

A third disciple entered the room and said, "To understand the meaning of things I take another perspective to see beyond the things themselves. There is a vacuum that contains everything, the whole. Individuality ends in a vacuum, which constitutes a unity. That unity is broken down

---

[23] Tathata is synonymous of dharmata. It may be translated both as "suchness" and "thusness" (sometimes "thingness", but it seems uncertain). Brosse (1999) suggested, as synonymous, the term "*sicceitas*", i.e., the being-thus of thing. In fact, like "*haecceitas*", it comes from Latin, where "*sic*" implies "thus" and, hence, "thus thing". Tathata represents the true nature of things as they are. In Suzuki (1977, vol.3, p. 99) and Watts (1957, p. 82) it is translated as Suchness. The terminological difficulty is evident in the text as Bashu interrupts the disciple twice as he was speaking.

into many different entities, that return to the origin in a circular motion. I look at an object and see it as it is, in its suchness or thingness.

Then, I look at it again and it is something else, it takes on a life of its own and arouses feelings because it is that object, and not another. It is a revelation. In contemplation, sensations become emotions that are in a relationship with things. Their changes over time undermine feeling, but the feeling remains in the memory."

"There is no sense in what you are saying," Bashu interrupted him.

"Is that because you do not see it?" Bashu tried to place his *keysaku* on the disciple's shoulder, but he moved away, avoiding it. Then came a blow to the ankle that made him tumble to the ground.

"Do you want me to talk about the meaning of life now?" he growled from the ground.

"Yes. Tell me about it," Bashu insisted.

"There is no meaning of life if you do not look for it, and you do not find it if you look for it. When you find it you have lost your life, and when you lose it, you find it." Bashu pressed him. "Are you here because you escape from life or because you are searching for life?"

"If I think about the life of my peers, who stayed behind in the village, I have escaped. If I think of the life that I want, then I am searching for life, but I am still far from the goal."

"The goal is within reach, but you are still not there. When you are close, it will be far away from you. When you reach it, you will have lost it. It will soon be dawn. Get up and go away."

The fourth disciple came in and said, "When you are growing up, it seems endless. Then, after you reach maturity, it ends quickly and then you face decline. Can we find a meaning in decline? No, we cannot find it. Melancholy overwhelms me. Time passes and everything goes away in the wind and water. Everything deteriorates over time. All changed, changed utterly: A terrible beauty is born."

"Are you in decline?" Bashu asked.

"In some senses. Time passes and everything seems useless." Bashu interrupted him. "Look at your face: A young man is turning into an adult. The truth is that everything is being transformed."

"That does not comfort me. I did not want to follow my peers, but I feel a strong bond with the world, with the sky. I need serenity that I do not find. I seek harmony. I do not want to turn back, but I do not know where to go."

"Stand where you are and meditate. Listen to the words coming from your heart. Follow the images that flow before your eyes. Follow them to get away from them. When the time comes, you will know how to recognize it. You will cross to the other side. *Svaha*." The disciple wanted to continue talking, but it was time to go and he took his leave with a bow.

The fifth disciple entered. It was Okano. A grimace appeared on the face of Bashu, who spoke first, "Why have you come? The meaning of things does not regard you because everything is already predetermined for you Christians with your doctrine of predestination. Life is a punishment: *"Accursed is the ground for your sake, with hard work you will derive nourishment from it, you shall earn your bread with the sweat of your brow. Dust you are and to dust you will return"* (Genesis 3.17-19).

"Predestination or not, the afterlife is a mystery, like the present life."

"No," Bashu answered firmly. "The afterlife is determined by your Faith. The present life is only a transition to the afterlife. Comply with the Law and you will receive your reward. The meaning of your life is this."

"It is not enough to comply with the Law to get the reward. It is necessary for the Law to change your life, here and now. Your reward is this: To live the Law in accordance with your intellect, will, and heart, without thinking about the Law, and to be happy."

"Is your reward no more than this?"

"It is the encounter with the Truth and you cannot describe it in words. If you meet it, it is a revelation of beings and things. If you welcome it, it transforms you. If it does not transform you, it has gone away and you have missed an opportunity. The meaning of life is in this transformation, in this change that takes place in you, leading to happiness."

"But are you happy when you suffer?" Bashu asked, swinging the *keysaku*.

"Faith must come before the reason, but reason has to do without faith. We are here, halfway across the river. Sometimes the water is pleasant and makes us dream, other times it is cold and benumbs us. It is sometimes tumultuous and shakes us to the core. This is where I have to swim. I need to learn how not to drown and you can help me."

"I tell you that you will drown all the same," Bashu said swinging the *keysaku* again.

"Whatever will be, will be. I will go under but then float back to the surface."

"Is the meaning of life dependent on this hope? You will not return to the surface." The *keysaku* stopped swinging and Okano was bewildered for a moment. He fell into a trance. When he recovered he spoke in a low voice, responding to the final argument of Bashu. "Then I will have learned what life is." He untied his shoes, took off them, and clasped his hands in prayer.

"What are you doing with those shoes?" Bashu asked him with his *keysaku* pointing at Okano's chest.

"I need to take good care of them in order not to lose them."

"*The sharp instruments of the state cannot be shown to the people*" (Laotse, XXXVI, 1982, p. 90) he said and dismissed him with two blows from the *keysaku*, one on each shoulder.

67. Life and death

One day Bashu asked Okano. "Is the Son of God alive?"
Okano immediately replied, "Every day he is among us."
Okano responded. "Then he is dead," and went away. Okano
knew he had a new problem to reflect on: life and death,
centred on the difference between the place where he was
and his place of origin. In the beginning, the death of God
redeemed us all, opening the doors of the afterlife and
reducing the fear of death through the resurrection of the
body and the soul. God had come down to earth to live and
had suffered as a man though more than a man. In this story
man's presumptuousness is clear, as man had made himself
in the image and likeness of God at the centre of creation
ruling over nature, the sole beneficiary of salvation. Dogs,
cats and other creatures also had the right to live and survive.
Were they not also created for the greater glory of God? Was
not the butterfly the most wonderful of insects? What were
the limits of salvation? Animals too had the right to live, but
this was not part of his religion.

Only one species was saved because their members
possess consciousness. If humans ate meat, it was obvious
that they suppressed a being similar to themselves. It was
often a mammal: a pig, rabbit, lamb, goat or horse. If he had
been vegetarian, he would still have been a predator because
plants were living things too and they had the right to thrive:
A lamb had no more rights than a blade of grass. The tragedy
of existence was to be seen in the conflict between species:
the seagull fishing for anchovies, the snake attacking the rat,
the thrush devouring the butterfly, the hawk snatching the
thrush, the lion ripping the gazelle to pieces, the gazelle
grazing on the grass of the savannah, the grass absorbing
substances from the earth and the sky.

It was not enough to focus on human beings because the
whole world was to be loved, but love was debased due to

the need to survive, the need that took possession of the body and the mind. Why was there any need to eat or dress? Would it not be better to live without these needs? Without needs, human beings would be able to concentrate on the enjoyment of the beauty of things, capturing and consuming them. Theology did not address these inconsistencies, because it denied them: dogs, cats and other creatures simply had no soul and were not part of God's kingdom. He avoided thinking about theology, but could he ignore the theory of the knowledge of life? Life on earth was not important in itself, because His Word was the Way, the Truth and the Life (John 14.6).

"If he were alive, would the nature of the message change?" No, it would not, so it seemed to him, because the Word continued to live in its intrinsic brightness.

"And if He had not died?" It seemed that salvation did not necessarily imply his death, but only his origin. The commandment, "Love one and another as I have loved you" (John 13.34), a milestone in thinking and action, but it was not proof of being alive or dead[24]. By dying for all humanity, his death had been the greatest gift, even if neither His life nor His death were necessary because love was not measured by death, but by the immensity of His heart. Okano's mind was constantly immersed in these thoughts.

One day Bashu appeared and asked him again point-blank. "Dead or alive?"

"Alive," he replied in a decisive manner.

"I say to you, no,"[25] Bashu replied, with a disapproving tone.

---

[24] The quotation from John (13.34) may appear out of place here but it was chosen because it is represented a step forward from the received wisdom. The most radical expression is the following: "You shall love your neighbour as yourself" (Matthew 22.39, Mark 12.31, Luke 10.27), even if this concept was stated in the Old Testament (Leviticus 19.18).

[25] This may appear similar to the Case LV: Tao-wu and Chien-yuan visit a family to mourn the dead, in the Pi-yen-chi or "*collection of*

"Dead," Okano retorted to him, changing response.

"I say to you, no," Bashu insisted.

"Why do you not say so then?" Okano retorted vehemently.

"I tell you I said no," Bashu repeated patiently. "No one is dressed better than the lilies of the field (Matthew 6.28, Luke 12.27)," and left him.

Okano continued to reflect on the question, but he could not find a suitable way. He floundered around with no way out. He was dead and his life was hidden with Christ in God (Paul, Letter to the Colossians 3.3) and for this reason he was the Nazarene.[26]

Did he live by dying? And was he alive as he was dead? It was not a *koan*, but it was as if it were. The reasoning did not stand up to critical scrutiny. He did not feel able to penetrate the Word, to probe the mystery of life that merged with the mystery of death. He resisted undaunted by the exhaustion of the body, because he knew that the point was there, in that journey to the edge of existence. He was behind and beyond the border. To live and to die are in the continuous present: if you enlighten yourself, you live; if you live without enlightenment, you die. To die, then, is also to live. Bashu met him while he was immersed in this swirl of thought, and Bashu asked him again. "What do you say if I tell you that he is alive and dead?"

---

green rock". This consists of poetic comments of Hsueh-tou of one hundred cases drawn mainly from the history of the Zen Masters, entitled "*The Transmission of the Lamp*" (Suzuki, 1977 vol, 2, pp. 235-245). The similarities are more apparent than real because the frame of reference is different.

[26] The attribute Nazarene seems not due, as is often supposed, to Nazareth, which apparently did not exist even in the time of Jesus. There are various hypotheses. One hypothesis is that it comes from "natzar", which means secret, hidden; this is the underlying meaning here (Craveri, 1990, p. 514).

He felt equal to the challenge. "When you speak to me, that is your teaching. When I should speak to you, I have nothing to say."

"Whatever you say is wrong," Bashu concluded definitely, disappearing out of sight.

Okano never tired of thinking about death, which was the necessary step for life, rather than a reincarnation through transformation or rebirth in the perennial changing of states: flowers perished to produce fruit, fruit decomposed to leave the seed in the earth, seed rotted for the plant. The plant flourished, bore fruit, and died to return to earth. It was the endless cycle of existence that could be considered immanent, inevitable, and without end. Everyone was trying to get out to follow the path that rose to the sky. Enlightenment was the other key to opening the door beyond the perennial cycle of matter in the making, but it was not the exclusive right of a system or a *bodhi*.[27]

It was a personal state that opened the eyes on the truth, because only by flooding eyes with light do we discover the relationship with the things of the world, getting in touch with the ultimate and eternal reality. The joy of the present was the key to being, just as one was, and to walk down a street that transcended appearances.

The necessary and the unnecessary merged into a single indissoluble entity, inherent in the development of the world and the essence of reality. Fullness and the emptiness, being and nothingness, were identical and complementary elements, the negative and positive stretching across the infinity of the whole, and God was the whole. He felt he had achieved maturity, a new man in new clothes, with a new appearance, but still the same. In essence, however, he was

---

[27] "Bodhi" literally means "awakening" and denotes access to the non-dualistic way of thinking, the realization of supreme wisdom (prajna), the revelation of the "original face". "Bodhisattva" literally means "to be awakened", the one who, upon awakening, renounces the final liberation (nirvana) to help other beings to be free (Brosse, 1999, pp. 211-212).

different, the result of an inner transformation. There were no words to describe it, he saw it, felt it, perceived it, and human language could not describe it. The meeting took place with the sign of Jesus, with death and life, as expressions of a unified existence as he felt alive and dead at the same time.

Bashu appeared along the path, while he was immersed in these thoughts. Okano stopped and began to walk backwards remaining in front of Bashu.

"What are you doing?" Bashu asked him.

"I am walking in the footsteps of the dead."

"You are out of step. You are walking in the footsteps of the living," Bashu rebuked him.

Okano started walking sideways like a crab, and replied to him. "The dead and the living coexist and are blowing in the wind."

"The wind bends the branches of the olive tree, but the clouds follow it in the sky. Where are the clouds of your thoughts?" Bashu asked him enigmatically. Meanwhile Bashu approached him and stood directly in front of Okano. Bashu took Okano's hands, his left hand in Okano's right hand and his right hand in Okano's left hand, and moved in a swaying motion with him, as if in a dance. Okano responded, staring into his eyes. "The living and the dead sleep in the sky, they lie on the ground, they walk on water, they revive with fire."

Bashu let go of Okano's hands and turned round, taking his place at Okano's side and following him in his crab-like footsteps. After, Bashu came back in front of him, taking Okano's hands in his again. After a few steps together, Bashu left him with his left hand free, then he grabbed the *keisaku*, struck a blow on each of Okano's shoulders, and walked quickly away.

68. Theology lesson

"I would like a meeting, not a *mondo*, to talk to each other openly and clearly, not allegorically, but with a view to achieving harmony; not in figurative words, but in congruent terms," Okano asked Bashu.

"You need to gain awareness of the limit of thought in relation to infinity but it is an illusion. Your question is wrong and will lead you into conflict with the world."

Okano insisted. "I think it is time to talk clearly. The sun is low on the horizon, dusk will soon be here and the sailors will sail back into the harbour."

"Yes," Bashu agreed. "Your stay here is coming to an end. You have no chance, you know, but I will bestow this favour on you equally as a gift of impending separation. Choose your topic."

Okano then laid his cards on the table. "Evil."

"The one who knows does not speak. The one who speaks does not know. But you want to talk, so do so."[28]

"Birth and illness, pain and anguish, decline and death are sorrow and evil. Sometimes evil comes from others, sometimes from within. This evil is understandable, because it is the need for freedom as we have the chance to do or not to do something. There is a limit to the restrictions we can place on those who intend to commit evil."

Bashu interrupted him, saying, "You are just at the First Noble Truth: Life is *duhkha*."[29]

---

[28] "*Those who know do not talk/ those who talk do not know/ close the mouth/ shut the doors/ blunt the sharpness/ unravel the knots/ dim the glare/ mix the dust/ this is called Mystic Oneness ...*" (Laotse, LVI, 1982, p. 123).

[29] The term "duhkha" indicates the great evil of the world, suffering as an essential characteristic of existence that the method of Buddha (dharma) overcomes (Watts, 1957, p. 62).

Okano smiled, bowed his head out of respect, then he went on. "There is evil that comes from inside and we are powerless before it and we have no reasons for its existence, as in the case of a disease or a disfigurement. In these cases we cannot understand the reason for its existence, and we cannot accept the consequences. It is not easy to overcome."

"Are you disfigured?" Bashu interrupted him.

"No, I am not."

"Then, let those who are disfigured tell us how it is because they may be perfectly at ease with their disfigurement. If they did not accept it, they would be entitled to protest, although protest itself is *duhkha* because *duhkha* is frustration also. The right to live a normal life (but what is normality?) is undermined. Thus, implicitly, we are at the Second Noble Truth: The avidity for life (*trishna*) is *avidya*, which means ignorance and unconsciousness. Evil is hard to explain. We follow the *dharma* to free ourselves. Those who are not able to do so will remain a victim of their *karma* and will continue to be tied to the wheel of *samsara*[30]. In your system, you free yourself only by means of faith after making the transition from life to death. Someone has paved the way for you. This means there is no way to achieve awakening and to see good and evil in emptiness, permeating our whole existence."

---

[30] Karma literally means action and represents the law of universal causality according to which every action produces a fruit, which ripens over a certain period. It is characterized by its imperishability or indestructibility (avipranasa), i.e. non-decay or non-disappearance, so that the consequences are to be seen in this life or in a subsequent life. This connects karma to samsara. See Suzuki (1977, vol.2, pp. 250-260).

Samsara means migration and indicates the cycle of birth and death that are generated endlessly, the one from the other, and from which one can escape only with the final liberations that one can achieve by playing an active role to reach final freedom (nirvana) through meditation.

"If you want, '*let this cup pass me by*' (Matthew 26.39, Luke 22.42). Faced with the obstinacy of evil, the existence of an entity to represent it seems likely, in the same way as those who represent good. Obviously, we are talking about God and the Devil, Light and Darkness." With an expression of surprise and disapproval, Bashu replied. "This struggle between good and evil is ever present in our reasoning, but unity is the generating principle of the world, not duality or multiplicity, arising from the discriminatory mind. Reality can only be understood in an intuitive way, and not in a rational way. In the Upanishads[31] it is written: "*Where knowledge is without duality, deprived of action, cause or effect, inexpressible, incomparable, beyond all description, what is it? It is impossible to say!*" (Watts, 1957, p. 50).

"Understanding is necessary because ignorance is darkness, blindness and lack of awareness."

"Your God possesses all the finest qualities to the highest degree. He is infinite, unlike our finitude in time and mind. How can we fully understand the designs of his creation?"

Okano continued. "We cannot, but if we cannot understand, believing becomes difficult because it is only a matter of faith. Can someone persuade somebody else to have faith, without rational evidence?"

"It says in the Bible: '*How blessed are those who never saw me and yet have found faith*' (John 20.29). The reasoning does not go very far, because the finite cannot contain the infinite. Reflect for a moment on the numbers. What do we know about natural numbers?"

"They are infinite."

"Even numbers and odd numbers?"

"They are both infinite."

"And relative numbers?"

"They are infinite too."

---

[31] The text was translated from Italian, originally translated from an English text, reported in Suzuki as cited by Watts (1957).

"Relative numbers are both positive and negative, and are all the same infinite. Is it not a mystery to the mind? Good and the evil are similar to positive and negative, in the same order of infinity. Could they co-exist in the same body? We do not know because we are ignorant. We persist in separation; perhaps, we must insist on the unity of being. We persevere in judgment based on our limited vision, but we must go beyond our limits to see the ultimate reality. Going beyond our limits depends on enlightenment and all our efforts are directed to this end. You call it the ultimate vision of faith, the light of the world, the ecstasy of your love for God who illuminates all things. If you do not see it, you cannot talk about it. That is what it is all about. When you see it, you no longer need to ask questions. You talk about it because you want to see it? We Buddhist are philosophers, like many others, but above all pragmatists. We appeal to experience (Suzuki, 1977, vol. 2, p. 219), not to rational description, because only those who go through fire are purified. Those who only describe it will not purified. Only those who go across the abyss can appreciate the harmonious unity of reality. Even the student of Zen must have great faith, because only those with great faith can support the trials to which they are subjected, the sacrifice and perseverance, which are required by the path. Zen is always a matter of life and death in every act and in all circumstances. Faith does not exempt you from an active role and discipline helps to open your mind. In Zen believing is not only being, but also becoming. Becoming gives rise to existential dissatisfaction, a restlessness that releases the flame of transformation. Religion wants only to be, and to believe is to exist (Suzuki, 1977, vol. 2, p. 278) in the acceptance of good and evil. *When I am completely united to You with all my being, pain and sorrow will not exist for me.* (St. Augustine, Confessions, 10. 28.39, translated from the Catechism of the Catholic Church, p. 31). You have been warned by saints and mystics that we must not construct a concept of God, because it is not possible to describe a perfect body with the imperfection of our words."

"St Thomas Aquinas teaches that we cannot grasp God by what He is, but only by what He is not (St. Thomas Aquinas, Summa contra gentiles, 1.30, from the Catechism of the Catholic Church, p. 31). I fear that what 'He is not' cannot be fully grasped. We cannot understand how He cannot be what He is not, because otherwise we return to the dichotomy of good and evil. If He embodies only good, then where does evil go? God is all and above all. Whatever He is, whether one or many, He is All."

"What of emptiness?" Bashu interrupted him.

"If God is whole, then he is also emptiness."

"But is He above or inside emptiness?"

"If God were above emptiness, emptiness would not be empty any more, because there is someone or something that it contains. God is emptiness and the whole, because the whole is also emptiness and emptiness is necessarily everything. Note that I have not said: 'God is all and nothing'." (Suzuki, 1977, vol. 2, p. 318). Bashu bent down with a large circular gesture of his right hand. After a deep breath he said, "The candle has burnt out but the flame is renewed, and it multiplies in intensity and size."

"God is all and we are only a speck of dust. We can only attempt to embrace the whole, which is in the infinite emptiness of that tiny speck of dust. So, we can only persevere in our weakness."

"We can only persevere in our weakness," Bashu said interrupting him. Okano knew that if the master repeated the sentence of a disciple, he was inviting the disciple to reflect upon the question and was advising him that the *mondo* was coming to an end. However, Okano tried to carry on the conversation.

"Weakness is a fertile ground for faith."

"The fertile ground for faith is weakness, but discipline is what makes it grow. Where is the weakness in discipline?" Bashu asked.

185

"A plant grows even without fertilizer."

"Yes, a plant grows without fertilizer and it returns its fruits to the ground when they are ripe. Look! Even the seeds of the sun are falling on the horizon."

Okano became aware that the discussion was over. "The fire in the sky will come back tomorrow morning and the seeds will germinate with peonies in the garden." He bowed deeply and took his leave.

69. Meditating on the face of God

One day Bashu took Okano aside and asked him to meditate on the face of God. Okano reacted with surprise and dismay. "It is blasphemy. You cannot meditate on the face of God without outraging Him." Bashu replied. "Then do it without outraging Him."

Okano retired and began intense meditation, rejecting any reasoning, thinking about an image without a face, sculpting the emptiness around him, but he was aware that the book of Genesis said: "*Let us make man in our image and likeness*" (Genesis 1.26). This meant that the face of God was ours. What then was the face of God? Okano was so immersed in thought that he could not stop, he could not give up, he could not think why the origin and the end was in that face, in that fixed idea. He fell into a state of prostration and frustration: his eyelids remained wide open and his body remained motionless, he lost all feeling in his legs and he was floating in the air. With the passing of time, his body became as hard as stone, and all tactile sensation vanished. He lost all feeling in his chest. He felt his head detached from his body which was floating in the air, and the rest of his body was like dust in the sky among the colours of the rainbow.

One of Bashu's disciples became alarmed by his condition. He shook and lifted him from the position of meditation and asked, "What are you doing in this state?"

"I am trying to realize the vision of God," he answered in a state of bewilderment.

"What do you mean by realizing the vision of God?" the astonished disciple retorted. Okano was left dazed and confused. He did not know how to answer the question, but the disciple tried to help him. "Do you mean you are contemplating the face of God? Think of your heart and cast aside this idea."

Okano returned to meditate with his heart beating fast and with renewed energy. All through the day he imagined the face of God on the objects he touched. He looked up at the changing face of the moon, and even that was the face of God. It was always the same, visible and invisible, hidden and in sight, but he embraced the moon in his heart and cast it aside. The stars shone in the night sky and had the face of the universe, but he absorbed them in his eyes and cast them aside. During the day he worked hard until he broke into a sweat, as if in a state of delirium.

Suddenly he believed he had caught a glimpse of a beautiful face bathed in light, so bright that the brightness faded the features of the face, yet he saw perfectly the sweetness of the eyes, the delicacy of the features, the power of the gaze, the splendour of the smile. The vision was like the blossoming of the lotus flower, the drop of dew that miniaturized the universe, the lightning that lit up the immense night sky. He had found the answer. He rushed to Bashu's room, knocked, and just as Bashu opened the door he told him impassioned and spirited, "Here I am." Bashu held him at arm's length, saying, "Wherever you are, you are still distant" and slammed the door in his face.

He had to start all over again, not from the beginning, but rather from the end. He devoted himself humbly to the tasks that the community asked him to attend to. In a disciplined manner he focused on anything and everything, on the full and empty, on being and nothingness. He found himself suspended above an abyss, clinging to the root of a tree that could break at any moment. He had no appetite. He did not sleep. His attention strayed. He wasted away. Then Bashu called him. "Where are you?"

"I am here close to and far from everything, because I do not see anything, but the face of God is in all of us. His face is ours and ours is his," he said absent-mindedly. Then Bashu swung his stick in front of Okano's eyes. Okano was hypnotized. After a while, Bashu brought him round and said. "You are making progress but you should explain why the face of one is the face of many and the faces of many are one. We say that all things can be brought back to God, but where does he God come back to? This is the dilemma to be solved," (Suzuki, 1977, vol. 2, p. 84). Okano was surprised at these words, which reflected the core of his meditation, and said to himself, "Here, it seems to me that everything will come back to a question posed in the last century. Is the face of all the faces still a face?[32] It is a matter of circularity, there is no answer, but you can solve it as a postulate."

"What is a postulate?"

"A conventional truth."

"What do you do with a conventional truth, when you look for the absolute? The purpose of meditation on the face of God is that God is your mind. Do not tell me this is blasphemy. Do not tell me that God is infinite and cannot be contained in the finite of your mind, as some theologians claim. The problem is your mind. What is it? Look where the face of God is conceived. Concentrate on *who*. Who is the person who wants to see his face and all faces? Is it the mind? Is it the body? Is it matter? Is it God? Or none of these? Then *who*? Meditate on this with serenity and trust, without a goal, with the goal to go beyond the goal, forgetting it and living day-to-day (Suzuki, 1977, vol. 2, pp. 134-135). This meditation is similar to the *koan* of your original face, which is the same for everyone and even for that of God. Circularity is in all things and reasoning is lost in the spiral that leads to the truth. You have to turn around or follow the spiral to find the exit. This is the meaning of going beyond the goal: the transcendence of appearance, the

---

[32] There appear to be similarities with Russell's paradox, also known as Russell's antinomy. In more formal terms, let any definable collection be a set. Let S be the set of all sets that are not members of themselves. If S is not a member of itself, then the definition implies that it must contain itself, and if it contains itself, then it contradicts its own definition as the set of all sets that are not member of themselves. It may be assumed that the set of faces is not in itself a face and is not a member of itself.

free fall from the sky, the leap into emptiness. The precipice is the desire to see, to come into direct contact with the object of thought, to eliminate all the barriers interposed between the subject and the object. It is a physical and mental effort that means opening the eyes to the truth. It is like the unfolding of the flower in the sun, like seeing everything in a speck of dust. The mystery of birth and death and the place before birth and after death disappears because you are on the top of the one and the other. This happens and when it happens you are awakened from ignorance, *bodhi*, and you have reached enlightenment. I warned you of the impossibility of reconciling your Christian beliefs with meditation and with the outcome of meditation because the meaning of work is supported by the idea of breaking dualistic schemes of understanding. If you do not understand this goal, because you know your origin and the end of your life, there is no reason to discover it and overcome it. As a result there is no reason to meditate to find or to get over it. That is why you have to ask, when you see beyond the circularity of life on earth, where are you exactly? Are you in heaven? Are you in mystical union with God? Are you at the resurrection of the flesh? You miss the underlying vision, the awakening that takes you back to the truth, but it is up to you to find the sense of immutability. It is up to you to experience the fusion with the beyond. You must follow the road to the end, and it will bring you back to your starting point. You have arrived at the end of anything and everything. *Gate, gate, paragate, parasamgate, Bodhi, svaha.*"

He did not allow him time to reply, because he put his left hand over his mouth and with his right hand dangled his stick in front of Okano's eyes. Finally, he twisted his left ear, as if to awaken him from a slumber. Okano exclaimed, "Master, you hurt me," but Bashu had turned and was walking away.

The next morning, when Okano went to the kitchen, Bashu suddenly appeared to him saying, "Okano, where are you?"

"I slept well last night," he answered with a gentle smile.

"Do you want to talk about the meditation on the face of God?" Bashu continued with an urgent tone. Okano raised his hands to the sky and said to him, "Before I only listened with my ears. Now I also see with my ears."

70. Thinking of the transfiguration

One day Bashu took Okano with him and led him to the most secluded part of the garden. He invited him to sit on a bench, then they sat down in silence, as if inspired by the peace of the place. Suddenly Bashu said to him, "If transfiguration is reality, then what is the reality?" Okano looked at him intently and, after a few moments, answered. "When I dream, I am awake. When I am awake, I sleep." Bashu stretched his hand out towards the sunset as if suggesting to contemplate it, "Look, the sun is awake and going to sleep," and, after a moment, he added. "It is time to wake up to the touch of Jesus on Mount Tabor" (Matthew 17.1-8, Mark 9.2-8, Luke 9.28-36). Okano looked surprised because it was the first time he had mentioned Jesus to him, but Bashu was no longer there.

Jesus had taken his favourites to one side. All men should have been his favourites, but the Bible recounts that they were the favourites. This predilection was genuine and authentic. Jesus could show his true face only if it was beyond the line of shadow, he seemed as bright as the sun and his appearance changed, so that he became the face of all faces, the one and the many. The transfiguration was a vision of reality going beyond appearances. The evanescence of His figure was a sign of illusions behind the line of shadow. The light, the sweetness of his features, the perspective changed and all returned to the pre-existing reality, the truth without veils. If someone entered into a relationship with him, he went to the root of things and could feel fear, exultation and serenity. Fear was the reaction to the unknown and death, because being born in a new dimension implied dying in the present dimension and moving beyond futility. Fear vanished at the touch of Jesus because the relationship with the Truth gave man the strength to transcend it, to find the Way, and to see the Light.

This thought was his *satori*, a thought not expressly stated, contiguity without overlapping. In this view, there was no more discrimination between opposites, but only the acceptance of good and evil, right and wrong, virtue and vice, reward and punishment. Dualism vanished into unity. Everything flowed from this fusion: the exaltation of being in the world, the joy inherent in encounters and experience.

He experienced a syncretism and managed to reach an elusive truth in the darkness of the mind. One could not tell other people, though, because they would not have understood. In this inspiration he discovered in himself another person, he had turned into something still undefined, but he felt that he had overstepped a boundary. He could not go back because the balance was unstable, but it was the right way to continue. He needed not only faith, but the constant exercise of discipline to awaken feelings in the heart and to open his eye to the world around him.

This experience had to remain a secret. It made no sense to talk about it with others, because the truth could not be explained in words. He had to experiment with it and, if he did not cross the threshold of illusion, he would still be wrapped in the world of illusion. He started to shake uncontrollably, his heart beating fast and strong, his legs buckling beneath him, and he fell with a dull thud to the ground, like a ripe apple. He did not know how long he lay there in the garden. He felt Bashu shaking him and asking, "Where are you?"

"Before your eyes," he answered, completely dazed.

"Wherever you are, you are still far away. But however far away you are, you are already close to your objective." Bashu tweaked his nose with a soft touch, that was gentle and painful at the same time. Okano did not scream, but he closed his eyes for a movement, as if this was induced by a force beyond his will. When he opened his eyes, Bashu was no longer there and Okano did not understand what had happened. Perhaps he had been unconscious for a few seconds.

From then on, he persisted in his reflections with humility and perseverance. His strong determination strengthened his character, as he became more and more a free man with a free will, that is the essence of being. The effort he made to perform his tasks regenerated his mind and body.

One day he was in the garden in the secluded place to which Bashu had led him. The sky was dark and a storm was gathering, with thunder pounding his ears and lightning flashing across the night sky. He walked slowly homeward, but on the way the lightning struck a tree close to him, shaking him to the core of his being. He took a few more steps, then slipped in the mud and fell to the ground. He lay there dazed and stunned for a while. When he got up he felt as light as a feather. He fell with the raindrops, he flowed with the water of the streams, he swayed with the grass, he was born and died with the spring storm. He sat down at his table and wrote these verses.

Heavy storm
thunder and lightning in the sky
I make it home.

A flash on the face
I slip on the muddy
ground and lie there.

Awake or asleep
I experience the Light
of another life.

In every drop
I catch a glimpse of the rock
of my Way.

This is happiness
searching for
the Truth.
I dance in the mud
in harmony with the world
I lack nothing.[33]

The time has come
to return
where I came from.

Bashu materialized mysteriously behind him, with the *keisaku* at his waist and another one resting horizontally on the palm of his hand. Okano rose from his chair, inspired and moved, bowed low and silently thanked him for the gift: *hi shin den shin.*[34]

Bashu handed him the stick and said, "It is time to go. Our dress (*kesa*) is not your dress (habit), but a stick has its function, even as a companion. You will find it useful along the Way."

Okano took it in both hands and held it close to his heart, then bowed again and said, "It is not the dress that makes the man, but the stick which accompanies him. Today many

---

[33] Old Testament, Psalm 23, The Lord is my shepherd. The verse is: "*I shall not want*".

[34] In Japanese the phrase is "*kokoro kara kokoro*" and means "from my soul to your soul". The expression is used to indicate the mode of transmission from the Zen master to his disciple (Deshimaru, 1977b, p. 80). The meaning here is direct communication, without words, an empathic understanding typical of those who have achieved enlightenment. There can be no transmission to Okano, given his beliefs.

peach flowers have fallen and the ground has been embellished with the blossom."

Bashu raised his hands almost at shoulder height, palms facing the sky, and replied, pointing to the tallest tree in the garden, "The top of the sequoia penetrates the clouds of heaven."

Afterword

The name of Bashu, the protagonist, may be mistaken for a corruption of the name of the brilliant Japanese poet Matsuo Basho (1644-1694) who transformed *haiku* from comedy to high artistic expression. Basho was the pseudonym derived from the banana tree planted in front of his house (Scalise et al., 1996), whereas his real name was Munefusa. He was called *haijin*, the one who knows how to express emotions, feelings, the world and life through *haiku*. *Haijin* is one who has a high degree of sensitivity and a genuine love of nature, in its transience and mutability. He has had many followers and imitators. Basho was not a Zen master, though, the Bashu in this collection of stories is a Zen master and his name is intended to celebrate or commemorate a great Zen master. In fact, Bashu is a portmanteau term resulting from a blend of the name of Basho with Joshu, one of the greatest Zen masters: Joshu Jushin (778-897 BC). Joshu derives from a transcription in Japanese of his Chinese name, Chao-Chou Ts'ung-shen, but there are various transcriptions. He lived under the T'ang dynasty (Scott, Doubleday, 1992). The choice of the name Bashu is a reference to the *haiku* blossoms in Zen and the fact that Zen masters cultivate *haiku*. It is also a tribute to two sources of inspiration. The characters in these stories often conclude by expressing their feelings by means of classical *haiku* verses, though in the English version they are not always classical.

The title of the collection is reminiscent of that of other collections (including Brosse, 1999; Cleary 1993; Senzaki, Reps, 1957). The first part of the title expresses both the speculative nature of the stories and the recurring themes in the characters, who are always seeking a direction or an answer to an urgent question posed by themselves or by an interlocutor, generally the Zen master. The second part of the title indicates the number (70), the genre (Zen stories), and the spatial delimitation of culture (the West), reflected in the style of writing. The collection is not intended to describe the way of Zen for those who wish to practise it, but to cast light on some of the similarities with the Christian religion for those who wish to practise Christianity following a path of individual consciousness and mysticism. This is problematic, because it involves religious syncretism, which often entails unnecessary, artificial, and uncritical fusions, often implemented in relation to purely practical and personal needs.

Theory is for theoreticians, philosophy is for philosophers, stories are for storytellers reflecting on the ideas the storyteller intends to highlight. The principles in the stories are reflected in the billowing of clouds, the twittering of swallows, the howling of the wind, and the splashing of water. Stories may provide insights into mysticism and pantheism. They may combine different aspects of theory to achieve union with the Absolute or God, through asceticism and a strictly individual path, without the logical argumentation of an essay. This is perceptible, albeit obliquely, in the stories. However, it should be borne in mind that the definition of the conceptual issues in the stories should be left primarily to the philosophers and theorists.

The stories adopt stylistic features that are just the opposite of the spirit of Zen: dry and essential. The style is more in line with a Western dialectical tradition than a typical dialogue between a Zen master and his interlocutor. I wish to extend my thanks to my friend Andrea Ginzburg, who read an early version of the work, advised me to drain the stories, an image that fits well with the content.

Author: "To drain something, first it is necessary to flood it."

Andrea: "After flooding, you need the sun to dry it out."

Author: "The story is a place where you can dream, imagine, and think. It is the *topos* of the intellect of the soul, and it is a fountain from which to drink. What do you drink, if there is no water?"

Andrea: "Well, be careful not to drown where there is no water."

The contents of the stories were inspired by different situations often chosen by chance. According to the initial idea, mentioned above, the stories were intended to deal with various aspects relating to the Christian religion, reworked from an original point of view and infused with the spirit of Zen. The idea was ambitious but hard to achieve due to the inherent difficulties arising from the extreme diversity of the two religions and worlds. In any case, a comparative study would have required an essay not a literary text. Nevertheless, it was decided to take up challenge. There were numerous essays dealing with similarities and commonalities between Zen and Christianity (*inter alia*, Mazzocchi, Tallarico, 1994; Mazzocchi, Forzani, 1997). The choice fell on the literary format as it can be more expressive and as it allows greater freedom. Rigorous reasoning may well suffer, but the emotional impact is stronger, polysemous and nuanced. The stories deal more with fantasy than knowledge, more with syncretism than with holism, more with indulgence than with rigour, more with the superfluous than with the necessary. No attempt was made to avoid enigmatic or elliptical reasoning presenting ambiguities and paradoxes for the reader to work on.

The ground was uneven and the prose adapted itself to the circumstances. The object of knowledge was "emptiness" (*sunyata*), with thought vanishing into non-thought (Masini, 1988). It was a difficult transition and no-one knows if the metamorphosis was fully accomplished or not.

All texts, in general, are constructed and those presented here are no exception. The aim is to construct a plot that does not seem artificial, and yet we cannot escape from the artificial world that has been built. We live from artifacts, among artifacts, with artifacts. The stories collected here are full of artifice and they do not come from an inspiration. In fact, they are essentially conceptual. They are not based on intuition and, therefore, are not spontaneous or related to direct experience. In a negative sense it could be said that they are stories with an intellectual theme, but storytellers approaching Zen tend towards intellectualism, as Suzuki wrote (1950, p. 77). This does not imply that they are based purely on reasoning, as they also rely on intuition: "They are logical only in part, in the sense that they like to proceed thinking about things they do not understand, but their intellectual will is not, so to speak, as strong as it is in professional philosophers ... intellectuals ... not to the point of becoming easy prey to the will to believe" (Suzuki, 1950, p. 78). We do not quote this extract to justify any shortcomings, but to show that every story adopting a Zen approach is inspired by rational thinking that permeates its inner fabric.

The intellect cannot always provide an analytical representation of the truth, while intuition can go into greater depth. The contrast between intuition and rationality therefore comes to the fore. The epistemological process cannot be represented by logic alone, because reality is changing and inexhaustible. Reality partly eludes the understanding of the intellect, even though "the unknowability should not be referred to the field of logic, but rather in some other place where you create your visions" (Suzuki, 1977 vol. 3, p. 102).

Images, symbols and similes favour representation and understanding: They constitute the meta-logic of reality. As a result, Zen masters are mystics, but also poets and visionaries rooted in everyday life as "[they] always use concrete objects that surround them" (Suzuki, 1977 vol. III, p. 102). Their responses, regardless of the logical and theological context of Buddhism, are imbued with poetry, emotional intensity, and intellectual enlightenment. The apparent irrationality in many of the answers given by the Zen masters highlights the contradictions of rational understanding.

The aim of these stories was to go beyond rationality. In this connection mention should be made of four stories that are intended more than the others to achieve this aim. Story no. 38, *The Christian Monk*, attempts to dissect the controversial and the uncontroversial aspects of the two approaches to experience: Christianity and Zen Buddhism. In order not to adopt the style of an essay, it was decided to frame it as a story, although slow and cumbersome. Story no. 44, *Circular Ethics*, is characterized more than the other texts by exegesis and commentaries, like those studied at high school. It is a story written with the sole purpose of providing a synthesis of Christian ethics. Although developed in a simplified form, it addresses common questions on this topic. The first part is brief, dry and limited to abstract questions relating to the pursuit of the good. The second part replicates the structure of the other stories: dialogues and thoughts of the protagonist seeking the truth and an understanding of the self, which are less reminiscent of Zen and more reminiscent of psychology, at least in the sense of the pursuit of peace and tranquillity. Story no. 57, *Syncretism* is more closely related to the beginning of the current millennium with messages disseminated through the media. The theme of the relationship between good and evil, as in story no. 38, is addressed again in story no. 68, *Theology Lesson*, from a slightly different perspective, also with a view to concluding the collection of stories.

The reasons for writing these stories are manifold. The passion for the subject, the love of poetry, and the attempt to gain insight into the soul were the driving force, but also the desire to attain knowledge. We cannot rule out the existence of a subjective path in these stories.

Amateurism was another element that played a role. The amateur delights in his knowledge and is aware that he will never achieve completeness (Zimmer, 1957, p. 18). These stories do not deal with the issues in the same way as they would be examined in a philosophical work on Zen (or Christianity), but they suggest feelings and emotions that are evoked by Zen short stories. Everyone achieves a certain depth. *"Out of abundance, he took abundance, and still abundance remained,"* according to an old maxim of the

Upanishads (Zimmer, 1957, p. 20). Here we aim to represent situations to stimulate useful reflections.

The insights provided by Zen, to some extent gleaned from the existing literature and embedded in these stories, are not always evident. However, just when one does not expect to find them, they may be there and when one believes they are there, they may not be. The vision that yields insights transcends our mind and to gain understanding it is not enough to quench our thirst for knowledge. The mind is confined to a limited space and a partial overcoming of limitations takes place only if the mind represents the wisdom of the body. Understanding passes through the body. Experience is physical, but also the mind is physical. Experience generates a perspective, which leads to intuition or rather to insights situated beyond intuition and reason. Experience cannot always be expressed in words. Those who are sleeping and dreaming believe they understand, but they live the duality of time and eternity, reality and fantasy, immanence and transcendence. Writing can be a way towards an awakening, but not the Way.

The original stories were of a literary genre but they contained many philosophical passages, the translation of which presents many difficulties. Something was lost in the translation from the original, including the full meaning of the beautiful and complex expressions but at the same time something else may have been gained, in terms of the simplicity bringing the stories closer to Zen stories. Moreover, the original *haikus* were often translated without reproducing their metrical pattern, requiring three lines or verses, having five, seven, and five syllables, respectively. Finally, it should be noted that the page numbers in the references generally refer to the Italian edition of the books.

Note to the first edition in English

This edition in English was derived from the third Italian edition of these stories and revised by William Bromwich. I wish to extend my thanks to him for his painstaking editing, though any remaining errors or inconsistencies are the responsibility of the author. The first Italian edition of the stories was published in 2011 on the site ilmiolibro.it. In such cases, it is customary for authors to distribute copies of the book to their friends who have an interest in the topic. During the distribution of the first edition two interesting bibliographical references came to light: Knitter (2009) and Le Saux (2004), who discuss their spiritual experiences. Both authors are Christian. The first reference, Knitter, was suggested by my mother-in-law, Clara Guerzoni, who is an enthusiastic reader and critic of my writings. Knitter analyses Buddhism and illustrates the many points of contact between the two religions, such as Okano, a character in several of the Zen stories. The surprise comes at the end: Knitter becomes both Christian and Buddhist, while Okano remains Christian. Okano's choice is moderate, in a certain sense. He gains enlightenment and returns to his monastery, without formally becoming a Buddhist. The second author, Le Saux, a Benedictine monk living in India, penetrated the innermost sphere of Hindu spirituality and he was captivated by it. He stayed on in India, because "the awakening to God is not separable from the awakening to ourselves" (see preface by Arrigo Chieregatti) and a sense of place can encourage it and preserve it. The experience of Le Saux was examined in a recent study by Marco Vannini (2013) who carried out an analysis of the opposition between mysticism and theology (following on from his study in 2010). Here the issues are complicated and go beyond the limits of the present discussion. In previous stories everything is left to literary devices rather than to the rigours of philosophical reasoning, except for a few passages. In general, the focus was on the motion of the heart, recognizing that discipline is the means to achieve any goal, to educate the body and soul: *gate, gate, paragate, parasamgate, Bodhi, svaha*! (See note in the Prologue).

The possibility of bringing together Buddhism and other religions is often justified by the fact that Buddhism is not a religion, but rather a philosophy, because it has no God. As a result, it is possible for Buddhism to coexist with Christianity. Buddhism appears as a way to achieve spiritual perfection, but in its long history it has had developments implying that it could be considered a religion (Franci, 2004).

We now turn to the two most important issues among those dealt with or touched on in the stories in the present collection: the problem of method and the problem of good and evil, as they were the driving force in the writing of this book.

1. The problem of method

The problem of method was the inspiration and starting point for examining the relationship between the two religions. In the beginning, it was assumed that the method of meditation practiced by Zen Buddhism was superior to other methods and that Christianity did not have a true method. Today, this view continues to be put forward, in spite of numerous doubts.

The crucial point about method concerns the objective: Where should it lead? In Buddhism, meditation should lead either to salvation, which is liberation (nirvana), and an exit from samsara, or to awakening. The problem is that it may not succeed. In Christianity, is it possible to borrow that method, even with some adaptation, as understood in Zen meditation? The answer for conservatives and purists is that it is not. In their view, there can be no *rapprochement* or borrowing between them because the two types of meditation have different functions, methods and goals. This brings to mind the verses of T.S. Eliot in *Little Gidding* (1943, p. 79):

> *We shall not cease from exploration*
> *And the end of all our exploring*
> *Will be to arrive where we started*
> *And know the place for the first time.*

What should we achieve by means of a method in Christianity? Should we attain Faith? Should we obtain Grace? Should we learn to believe in God? Our efforts as Christians are all directed at achieving the reward, which is salvation, in the sense of paradise. In examining these efforts we can say that "they are practices, not methods, which postulate the respect for rules," as shown in the history of Christianity. The methods may be many, but they share several elements, some of which are questionable: (1) the *mortification of the body*, until self-flagellation; (2) *penance*, which falls under the mortification of the body; (3) the *fear of God* and therefore respect for the law; (4) *obedience* and again respect for the law; (5) *chastity*, but this is common also to Zen.

There are many methods (rules) in Christian teaching. Here we mention fours only: the first two are among the most popular, the third is often ignored, and the fourth is almost unknown.

1.1. Rule of St. Benedict

The Rule of St. Benedict (1980) is summarized with the motto "pray and labour" (*ora et labora*, in Latin), which elevates work to the spiritual status of prayer. It means that prayer should be work and work should be prayer. This rule is typical of Western culture, concentrating on doing rather than on being.

If we were to transpose this precept into Zen terms, we could say, "When you pray, you must be a prayer and when you work, you must be work."

The difference is evident: it is not a method to achieve something that relates to the state of being, but to gain something in the future, in the afterlife. It is a set of precepts that can help to achieve a spiritual dimension as a secondary effect, because the goal is virtuous behaviour, not a change of conscience on the inside.

If we see this as a way of salvation, conceptual distances would be reduced, but they would not disappear.

1.2. Spiritual Exercises of St. Ignatius

Note [1] of the work of St. Ignatius (1914, first annotation, p. 20 of the available PDF), states that *"by this name of Spiritual Exercises is meant every way of examining one's conscience, of meditating, of contemplating, of praying vocally and mentally, and of performing other spiritual actions* ... [Just as] *strolling, walking and running are bodily exercises,* [similarly we call spiritual exercises] *every way of preparing and predisposing the soul to rid itself of all disorderly tendencies, and, after it is rid, to seek and find the Divine Will as to the management of one's life for the salvation of the soul."*

Compared to the rule of St. Benedict, the spiritual exercises of St. Ignatius pay greater attention to psychology, meditation, and contemplation. Spiritual exercises *"use acts of the intellect in reasoning, and acts of the will in reasoning in movements of the feelings"*, but they are less directed towards a discipline of the body as a way to achieve specific goals. The practice of spiritual exercises comes much closer to the practice of Zen meditation and can lead more easily to an approach to God, similar to a kind of enlightenment, but such exercises are still far from the concept of the method, at least for the paradigmatic premises of spiritual exercises.

It may be said that this approach and Zen Buddhist meditation may be juxtaposed, that is to say, the method of St. Ignatius becomes comparable with the Zen method. However, we do not intend to explore the matter further as it goes beyond the confines of the present discussion.

1.3. Mysticism

Mysticism is an attitude of the spirit aimed at union with the Absolute, understood as God, the Soul of the World, reflecting the real, experiential knowledge of God. Mystical self-fulfilment is a direct experience and a fruition of the divine with which one aims to join. It has the following characteristics: (1) *the absence of a logical approach,* which excludes rationality and results in irrationality, (2) *annihilation of the Soul* in the Absolute: in Christianity the soul is not lost but rather in an intimate relationship, in direct contact with God, (3) *mystical impulse,* which involves withdrawing from the world and renouncing passion, (4) *ecstasy,* the state of the soul when it is in contact with the Absolute, by which we mean God for Christians, who seek Grace so that the soul can rise to God, (5) *ineffability* and even here for Christians Grace is necessary.

An approach to mysticism is to be found in the work of Dionysius the Areopagite (Greek Διονύσιος ὁ Ἀρεοπαγίτης), often referred to as the Pseudo-Dionysius, the author of ten letters and four dogmatic and mystical essays. The addressees of the letters were all personalities of the apostolic age, though scholars have established that they date back to the second half of the fifth century AD. These writings were intended to convert Neo-Platonists to Christianity. The universe was conceptualized as a triadic process of ascent (and descent), procession and conversion leading to purification, enlightenment and union.

Mysticism represents the practice and method closest to Zen, because it centres on religious education in which those seeking God or the truth abandon all their acquired knowledge and experience (Suzuki, 1977, vol. II, pp. 283-287), though this does not guarantee entry into the Kingdom of Heaven. This is because vanity, conceit, and narcissism prevent humans from entering into contact with the divine world. Also the self and the intellect are an obstacle: *"unless you change and become like children, you will never enter the Kingdom of Heaven"* (Matthew 18.3). The intellect does not grasp the thing itself, but represents the thing itself through images, references, explanations. In this process, the focus moves away from the individual towards speculation (Suzuki, 1977, vol. II, pp. 284).

Buddhism may be said to be more intellectual than Christianity, because it combats ignorance and tends to encourage understanding, albeit intuitive, of existence detached from supreme love, though there are strains of Buddhism which claim otherwise.

Mysticism is the ideal way to move closer to maturity, because it leads one to live in harmony with the divine, through love of the mind and body in synchrony with the truth (Suzuki, 1977, vol. II, pp. 287).

Mysticism has not always been favourably received, because the direct relationship with God undermines the principle of authority, based on the Truth from Christ. The Church has sought to be the Guardian of the Truth through the centuries, acting as a universal authority (Mancuso, 2011, p. 349).

In the following some mystics are cited with brief biographical notes.

Meister Ekhart (Johannes Von Ekhart Ochheim: 1260-1327/28), son of Eckhardus, dictus de Hocheim. He was a Dominican and the most important Christian mystic: "God is and is nothing else, because the total being is indefinable. It is the In-principle."

John Tauler (Strasbourg 1300-1361). Also a Dominican, he popularized the mysticism of Johannes Eckhart. The core of his mysticism was the doctrine of the *"visio essentiae Dei"*, the blissful contemplation of knowledge of the divine nature, borrowed from St. Thomas Aquinas, but he went further in believing that knowledge of God was attainable in this world as a perfect man.

Marguerite Porete. A French theologian and author of the *Mirror of Simple Souls,* one of the main sources of the medieval doctrine of the heresy of the *Free Spirit,* she was burned at the stake in Paris in 1310. She was associated with the Movement of the Beguines and the Movement of the Free Spirit.

Angelus Silesius (Johannes Scheffler, Wroclaw, 1624-1677). He argued that the essence of God was defined by love: God cannot love anything without worth, nor can God become an object of love for himself, but he can manifest his infinite being in a finite form. In other words, he can become Man. God and Man therefore become one.

1.4. Hesychasm

Hesychasm (Greek: ἡσυχασμός, *hesychasmos*, from ἡσυχία, *hesychía*, which means peace, stillness, tranquillity, rest, quiet, silence, but also loneliness, withdrawal) is a form of meditation developed in the mysticism of the Eastern Orthodox Church, i.e., it is an eremitic tradition of prayer, in the sense that it is practised by hermits. In tradition, hesychasm consisted of retiring inward by reducing contact with the senses, to achieve an experiential knowledge of God. With this meaning, it can be traced back to the fourth century. However, understood as "a particular psychosomatic technique in combination with the Jesus Prayer" (https://en.wikipedia.org/wiki/Hesychasm), it can be referred to as a sect, the Hesychasts.

The sect was founded in the eleventh century among the Byzantine monks of Mount Athos. The members of the sect aimed to achieve mystical union with the deity by concentrating on the navel, combined with breathing, *"compress the air which passes through the nose in order to suspend breathing and mentally explore the inside of your body in order to find the soul. In the beginning there is only darkness and a tenacious thick, persevering day and night in the practice of this occupation, you will find, oh wonder, a boundless happiness"* (Nicephorus, the Hesychast of the thirteenth century, cited in Brosse, 1999, pp. 193-209).

These practices are similar to those described in Zen Buddhism. For Hesychasts, meditation becomes a way to approach God, to enhance perception, and to reach a state of grace. In this state of conscience, the gift of the Word can multiply its effects on the body, action, feelings and reality.

2. The problem of good and evil

The problem of good and evil (ethics) is dealt with explicitly in some stories, and here we make just a few brief comments; see also Ricoeur (2009, p. 135-154). Here we outline five models or approaches, identified and organized according to a personal scheme.

2.1. The absolutist model has been described by Ricoeur (2009, p. 142). This model presupposes an omnipotent God who can get what He wants, so the model is that of the tyrant: "He who can stop evil, why does he not do so?" In that case He is an accomplice of evil or co-exists with it (Manichaeism).

The *difficulty*: Where evil is not prevented, there is a hostility towards God, because the experience of evil and suffering among humans often leads to a sense of helplessness. In the end this leads to rebellion against God.

The *consequence*: Rejecting the absolutist model, and hence the concept of omnipotence, undermines God as a perfect being, leading to Manichaeism. There is a contrast between the two original kingdoms (Light and Darkness, Good and Evil, God and Satan).

The *defence*: It is not possible to fathom the mind of God, nor do we have the power to distinguish good from evil. All this happens because we cannot accept that evil is an integral part of life. Job responded to his wife: "*If we accept good from God, shall we not accept evil?*" (Job 2.10).

2.2. The guilt model is based on the paradigm of an *omnipotent*, but also a *just* God. If there is evil, it comes from our own guilt and evil is allowed as a necessary step towards purification (Old Testament). In short, it is deserved. The idea of a punitive God in the Old Testament does not fit well with this model.

The *difficulty*: Where there is no obvious fault on our part, there may be a misunderstanding about the implications of evil. A punitive God lacks credibility and is in contrast with the teaching of Jesus.

The *consequence*: Rejecting the guilt model undermines the concept of the justice to God, with the same destructive effects as the rejection of the absolutist model.

The *defence*: It may not be possible to know what evil has been committed, as argued in certain passages of the Book of Job (Old Testament). Zophar says: "*Can you fathom the mystery of God, can you fathom the perfection of the Almighty? ... He surely knows which men are false and when he sees iniquity, does he not take note of it? ... If you have wrongdoing in hand, thrust it away, let not iniquity makes its home with you. Then you could hold up your head without fault, a man of iron, knowing no fear.*" (Job 11.7-15).

2.3. The reward model has always the paradigm of a *just and omnipotent* God, but also *good* for the faithful: "I am a good Christian, and as a result I am protected and rewarded." On the whole, the individual has deserved this for virtuous conduct. As a result, it is compatible with the guilt model, but the reward model starts form an opposite perspective.

The *difficulty*: What about other people? Does our heart not tremble in the face of the evil that afflicts others? Where evil is rampant, the implication is that anyone afflicted by evil is not a good Christian.

The *consequence*: Rejecting the reward model weakens the concept of the goodness to God, implying the rejection of the idea of Providence that defends the faithful, though the concept of Providence is not of biblical origin. The rejection of this model is at least as devastating as the rejection of the other models.

The *defence*: As in the case of the guilt model, individuals are incapable of knowing when and to what extent they are good Christians. It is said that the saint lapses into sin seven times a day. The statement is an adaptation from the Book of Proverbs (24.16): "*Though the good man may fall seven times, he soon rises up again.*" This appears to annihilate Man in the face of God.

2.4. The universal model assumes the paradigm of the *God of almighty love*, who is infinitely good for everyone, so it is an inclusive model. God will save all people, both good and bad, both Christians and non-Christians. There are words of comfort that God addresses to us at times of suffering. The challenge is to be able to hear those words. There is no answer to those who say, "There is too much evil in the world for me to believe in God." (Ricoeur, 2009, p. 144). In this connection, we can consider the remark by the Swiss Jesuit theologian Hans Urs von Balthasar (1986, 1987, 1997) about hell: "It exists, but it is empty." Albeit in different terms, this idea was to be found in Christianity from the beginning. In the third century, Origen developed the concept of *apokatastasis*, which meant the reconciliation with Christ after a period of suffering of those condemned to hell, whether human beings or demons. He founded a school of thought among the Fathers of the Church, but it was condemned by the Council of Constantinople in 543 AD.

The *difficulty*: This model is in contrast with egoistic and narcissistic behaviour, "I, who have worked so hard, am rewarded as much as another who has done nothing." This seems unacceptable, but one should reflect on the many parables in the gospel, in particular, the Parable of the Prodigal Son (Luke 15.11-32) and the Parable of the Labourers in the Vineyard (Mathew 20.1-16).

The *consequence*: Rejecting the universal model means renouncing the love of God and his goodness. It casts doubt on our salvation. Only eternity and nothingness will remain for human beings with no other horizon.

The *defence*: The reason justifying the model appears as a recurrent theme in the stories in the present book. The meeting with the Word (God) implies the need to change one's life and perspective, because there is joy in being what one is and does. Joy is not in comparison to someone or something. Once again a connection is evident with the Parable of the Prodigal Son and the Parable of the Labourers in the Vineyard.

The response of Paul Ricoeur (2009, p. 144) is: *"The death of the suffering servant on the cross breaks definitively the idea of a kind of remuneration payable to God. God does not want our suffering, but he does not have the power to prevent it."*

The universal model may appear unacceptable. However, the unacceptability of the model is attenuated only with a pragmatic attitude, more proactive and less reactive, more altruistic and less selfish, more welcoming and less exclusive, more trusting and less suspicious. The main objections to this model fade away if one follows the perspective of love, including all and forgiving all, welcoming everybody and anything.

Let us reflect on the words that Jesus uttered on the cross: *"Father, forgive them, for they know not what they do"* (Luke 23.34). From this quotation we may infer that forgiveness is to be granted by the Father. This is something to reflect on whenever we ask someone to forgive our sins. Yet this is only the surface of the question. In fact, the quotation reveals a high degree of consistency with the words that Jesus preached: *"But what I tell you is this: Love your enemies and pray for those who persecute you"* (Matthew 5.44). Therefore, there is no need to forgive anyone, because love conquers all. Jesus loved his persecutors and prayed for them. This is the mystery and the omnipotence of love, which saves anyone and anything. In this regard, mention should be made of an interesting variation of the Lord's Prayer in many Protestant Churches: *"And forgive us our trespasses as we forgive those who trespass against us"* (Matthew 6.12). In another translation the statement is, *"And forgive us our debts [wrongs], as we have [already] forgiven our debtors [those who have wronged us]."* Our forgiveness had already taken place, as emphasized by the adverb "already". In this we can see the essence of love, which is the foundation of the Word of Jesus and his teaching.

2.5. The paradoxical model assumes the paradigm of a God who is infinite in all dimensions, and includes the universal model. It cannot be reduced, then, to the finiteness of our mind, which is contained in God and contains God, contained in the world and containing the world, as God contains the World and is contained by the world. Evil is the result of discrimination, sometimes necessary to fit the action not only to what impulsive/ compulsive instincts dictate, but also to ethical principles. In a certain sense, evil is an immanent property of existence.

The *difficulties*: Evil coexists with good, albeit in complicated forms, implying a latent Manichaeism. As in previous models, there is a disintegration of the image of God and his futility, because He is powerless in the face of evil and, if present in the world, then He should inevitably be involved and thus somehow associated with evil. In this sense, the adjective "paradoxical" can be understood.

The *consequences*: The paradoxical model leaves unresolved what it has not solved.

The *defence*: The fact that evil cannot be suppressed, at a conceptual and empirical level, is assumed by the model, as a paradox. Other models have either eliminated it with an authoritative principle or they have ignored it, relegating it to the background.

In this connection it should also be noted that not all arguments about the mercy of God are well founded. For example, people often ask: "Where was God?" when heretics were burned at the stake, "Where was God?" when abominable actions were committed in the concentration camps, gulags, laogai and killing fields? (Mancuso, 2011). In our view, this is the evil done by man to the detriment of man: God can do nothing to prevent it. What could he have done? Unleash a firestorm against the culprits? Those who adopt this type of reasoning use it to make an emotional impact. In fact, this objection does not consider the free will granted to humans, that is implicit in the absolutist model. In this perspective, the underlying conception resembles the Garden of Eden, where all is well.

Another argument put forward by Mancuso (2011, pp. 112-113), concerns the *"suffering of the innocent caused by genetic disorders."* Here the situation is more critical. It may be possible to prevent genetic disorders only in the Garden of Eden, but not in the real world.

It is more difficult to find answers to the suffering and lethal diseases of children or to the ravages of nature. There are no rational answers and this can be seen from some of the stories in this book. A relevant argument is to be found in the book of Job and in St. Augustine's works: our finite mind can never comprehend an infinite entity and its understanding is limited by its finitude.

The restless mind is not content with this, because it needs something credible and defensible. There is, unfortunately, no acceptable argument about the existence of evil. One example among many: we can appreciate good because there is evil, i.e., we can discriminate and be aware, while those lacking in conscience commit evil through ignorance. As a result, without evil, how would one know good? Rightly, people do not want evil, which is suffering, disease, violence, humiliation, slavery, deprivation and death. As a result, restlessness, affliction, and torment will remain for them. Anxiety is the driving force for research, and for seeking explanations for the good. Those who engage in research of this kind live a life of love and authenticity, that are essential for serenity.

Bibliography

Ayoama Shundo (1990). *Utsukushiki hito ni*, Kosei Publishing Co., Tokyo. Italian translation (1994). *La voce del fiume*, Edizioni San Paolo, Cinisello Balsamo (Milan).

Boccaccio Giovanni (1976). *Il decamerone*, Salani, Florence.

Brehm Alfred Edmund (1983). *La vita degli animali*, BUR Biblioteca Universale Rizzoli, Milan.

Brosse Jacques (1999). *Zen et Occident*, Éditions Albin Michel S.A., Paris (France). Italian translation (2003). *Zen e Occidente*, Editrice Pisani, Isola del Liri (Frosinone).

Cleary Thomas ed. (1993). *Zen Antics: A Hundred Stories of Enlightenment*, Shambhala Publications, Boston, MA. Italian translation (1998). *104 Scherzi Zen*, Mondadori, Milan.

Costituzione apostolica, "Fidei Depositum" (1992). *Catechismo della chiesa cattolica*, Libreria editrice vaticana, Vatican City.

Craveri Marcello (ed.) (1990). *I Vangeli apocrifi*, Giulio Einaudi, Turin.

De Loyola Ignacio (1548). *Excercitia spiritualia*, IHS. English translation by Father Elder Mullan, S.J. (1914). *The Spiritual Exercise of St. Ignatius of Loyola*, P.J. Kenedy & Sons, New York. Italian translation and afterword by Giovanni Giudici (1998), *Esercizi spirituali*, SE, Milan.

Deshimaru Taisen (1977a). *La pratique du zen (suivi des Textes sacrés du zen)*, Éditions Seghers, Paris. Italian translation (1981). *Lo zen passo per passo (La pratica dello zen – Testi sacri dello zen)*, Casa editrice Astrolabio – Ubaldini, Rome.

Deshimaru Taisen (1977b). *Vrai zen*, Éditions Seghers, Paris. Italian translation (1993). *Il vero zen*, © SE, Mondadori, Milan.

Deshimaru Taisen (1983). *Le bol et le bâton*, Éditions Cesare Rancilio/ Zen Éditions. Italian translation (1991). *La tazza e il bastone*, SE, Milan.

Eliot Thomas S. (1943). *Four Quartets*, Harcourt Brace & Co., New York. Italian translation (1976). *Quattro quartetti*, Garzanti, Milan.

Franci Giorgio Renato (2004). *Il buddhismo*, il Mulino, Bologna.

Knitter Paul F. (2009). *Without Buddha I Could Not Be a Christian*, Oneworld Publications, London. Italian translation (2011). *Senza Buddha non potrei essere cristiano*, Fazi Editore, Rome.

Knowles E. (2009). *Little Oxford Dictionary of Proverbs*, Oxford University Press, Oxford.

Laotse (1982). *Il Tao-Te-King*, Laterza, Bari.

Le Saux Henri (2004). *Ricordi di Arunachala. Racconto di un eremita cristiano in terra hindu*, Messaggero di Sant'Antonio Editrice, Padua.

Mancuso Vito (2011). *Io e Dio. Una guida dei perplessi*, Garzanti, Milan.

Masini Ferruccio (1988). *Pensare il Buddha. Dialoghi alla maniera Zen*, Edizioni dello Zibaldone, Pordenone.

Mazzocchi Luciano, Tallarico Annamaria (1994). *Il Vangelo e lo Zen. Dialogo come cammino religioso*, EDB Edizioni Dehoniane, Bologna.

Mazzocchi Luciano, Forzani Jisō (1997). *Il Vangelo secondo Luca e lo Zen*, EDB Edizioni Dehoniane, Bologna.

Mumon (1957). *The Gateless Gate, 10 Bulls*, Charles E. Tuttle, Tokyo, transcribed by Nyogen Senzaki and Paul Reps. Italian translation (1980). *La porta senza porta*, Adelphi, Rome.

Ricoeur Paul (2009). Dieu n'est pas tout-puissant, Conversation avec Bertrand Révillon, *Panorama*, 340(1999), pp. 26-30. In Bianchi Enzo (ed.), *Paul

Ricoeur: la logica di Gesú, Edizioni Qiqajon, Comunità di Bose, Magnano (Biella).

San Benedetto (1980). *Regola*, Edizioni La Scala, Noci (Bari).

Scalise Mario, Mizuguchi Vici Folchi Atsuko, Vasio Carla (1996). *Haiku antichi e moderni*, Garzanti, Milan.

Scott David, Doubleday Tony (1992). *Zen*, Element Books, Longmead. Italian translation (1994). *Lo zen*, Xenia, Milan.

Senzaki Nyogen, Reps Paul eds. (1957). *101 Zen Stories*, Charles E. Tuttle Company, Tokyo. Italian translation (1973). *101 Storie Zen*, Adelphi, Milan.

Suzuki Daisetz Teitaro (1950). *Living by Zen*, Rider & Co., London. Italian translation (1996). *Vivere Zen*, Edizioni Mediterranee, Rome.

Suzuki Daisetz Teitaro (1977). *Essays in Zen Buddhism*, Rider & Co., London. Italian translation (1977). *Saggi sul buddismo Zen*, voll. 1-3, Edizioni Mediterranee, Rome.

Vannini Marco (2010). *Prego Dio che mi liberi da Dio. La religione come verità e come menzogna*, Bompiani, Milan.

Vannini Marco (2013). *Oltre il cristianesimo. Da Eckhart a Le Saux*, Bompiani, Milan.

von Balthasar Hans Urs (1986). *Was dürfen wir offen?*, Johannes Verlag, Einsiedeln. (1987). *Kleiner Diskurs über die Hölle*, Schwabenverlag AG, Ostfildern. Italian translation (1997). *Sperare per tutti. Breve discorso sull'inferno*, Jaca Book, Milan.

Watts Alan W. (1957). *The way of Zen*, Pantheon Books, New York. Italian translation (1976). *La via dello Zen*, 2nd edition, Feltrinelli, Milan.

Watts Alan W. (1957). *The Spirit of Zen*. Italian translation (1960). *Lo Zen. Un modo di vita, lavoro e arte in Estremo Oriente*, 2nd edition, Bompiani, Milan.

Zimmer Heinrich (1957). *The King and the Corpse. Tales of the Soul's Conquest of Evil*, Bellingen Foundation,

New York. Italian translation (1983). *Il re e il cadavere. Storie della vittoria dell'anima sul male*, Adelphi, Milan.

Biographic Note

Michele Lalla was born in Liscia (Chieti) in 1952. He graduated in Physics at the University of Rome in 1976. He has lived in Modena since 1976, where he teaches (social) statistics at the Marco Biagi Department of Economics. He has published book of poems in dialect and in Italian, novels, and essays.

The collections of poems in dialect are: *Storie vère o 'nventate* (Solfanelli, Chieti, 1983), *Scurciature de memorie* (Campanotto Editore, Pasian di Prato, Udine, 2001), and *Dê nche éune* (Campanotto Editore, 2012), including a revised version of the poems in *Storie vère o 'nventate*.

The collections of poems in Italian are *L'Eco del Silenzio* (Lalli, Poggibonsi, 1984), *Il Vagito della Primavera* (Lalli, Poggibonsi, 1985), *Treninternetviaggi* (Campanotto Editore, 2006), *Le cinque stagioni* (ilmiolibro.it, Gruppo Editoriale L'Espresso, Rome, 2012), *Vita in B minore* (ilmiolibro.it, I ed. 2011, II ed. 2013), *Giostra di haiku* (ilmiolibro.it, II ed. 2015).

The prose compositions are: *La condanna* (in «Premio Letterario – *Racconti inediti*», 2ª edizione, anno 2006, Circolo culturale Archeosofia, Modena, 2007), *Trovare il senso: 70 storie zen occidentali* (ilmiolibro.it, I ed. 2011, II ed. 2012) containing an Italian version of the Zen stories in this collection, and the novel *Andrò in America – I* (ilmiolibro.it, 2012).

Dialect poems appeared in: *Diverse LinguE* (*12*: 155-161/1993, *15*: 143-151/1996, *19/20*: 125-134/1998 – all slightly modified and reprinted in *Scurciature de memorie*); *Tratti* (Mobydick, Faenza *35*: 10-13/1994). Italian poems appeared in: *Frontiera* (supplement to *Gli immediati dintorni*, Bologna, *5*: 38-39/1997); *Origini* (La Scaletta, San Polo di Reggio Emilia, *39*: 73-74/1999); *ilfilorosso* (*51*: 7/2011).

His literary writings include: "*Risposte al* «Questionario per i poeti in dialetto»" (*Diverse LinguE, 16*: 19-28/1997) and reviews in *ilfilorosso* (*46*: 51-53/2009, *49*: 35-37/2010, *50*: 48-51/2011, *52*: 44-48/2012; *54*: 53-56/2013; *55*: 47-51/2013; *56*: 40-43/2014; *57*: 46-49/2014; *58*: 46-51/2015).